Agency at Work

MODERNITY IN QUESTION
STUDIES IN PHILOSOPHY AND HISTORY OF IDEAS

Edited by Małgorzata Kowalska

VOLUME 17

PETER LANG

Monika Baer (ed.)

Agency at Work

Ethnographies in/of Late Industrialism

PETER LANG

Bibliographic Information published by the Deutsche Nationalbiblithek
The Deutsche Nationalbibliothek lists this publication in the Deutsche Nationalbibliografie; detailed bibliographic data is available online at http://dnb.d-nb.de.

Library of Congress Cataloging-in-Publication Data
A CIP catalog record for this book has been applied for at the Library of Congress.

The funding for this project was granted by the National Science Centre, based on decision DEC-2013/11/B/HS3/03895.

This work has been reviewed by Agata Stanisz (Adam Mickiewicz University in Poznań).

Cover illustration: Courtesy of Benjamin Ben Chaim

ISSN 2193-3421 · ISBN 978-3-631-84609-4 (Print)
E-ISBN 978-3-631-85630-7 (E-PDF) · E-ISBN 978-3-631-85838-7 (EPUB)
E-ISBN 978-3-631-85839-4 (MOBI) · DOI 10.3726/b18576

Peter Lang – Berlin · Bern · Bruxelles · New York · Oxford · Warszawa · Wien

This publication has been peer reviewed.

www.peterlang.com

Table of Contents

Monika Baer[1]

Preface

Agency seems to be a somewhat problematic issue. On the one hand, it has been more or less explicitly situated at the very heart of the discipline of ethnology and social and cultural anthropology since its emergence rooted back in the nineteenth century.[2] On the other hand, this centered location made agency taken frequently for granted and therefore not the main focus of anthropological theorizing. This situation has significantly changed at the turn of the 1970s and the 1980s, when the broader turn toward theory of practice put human acting subjects at the center. As Sherry Ortner (1984: 144, 159) notes, at that time there was a growing interest in interrelated bundles of terms: "practice, praxis, action, interaction, activity, experience, performance" and "the doer of all that doing: agent, actor, person, self, individual, subject." The consequent approach focused on human agency was "unique in accepting all three sides of the [Peter] Berger and [Thomas] Luckmann triangle: that society is a system, that the system is powerfully constraining, and yet that the system can be made and unmade through human action and interaction."

In the following decades the above analytical perspective has been developed in many interesting ways. Certain universality of agency as

1 Department of Ethnology and Cultural Anthropology, University of Wrocław, monika.baer@uwr.edu.pl, ORCID: 0002-2415-1060.

2 Even though origins of contemporary versions of social and cultural anthropology can be usually traced back to the forms developed mostly in the UK and the USA, these were not the only trajectories along which scholarly analysis into human cultural diversity were historically evolving. In this context, European continental traditions labelled as ethnology should be taken into account as well (cf. Barth et al. 2005). Consequently, in this book we offer analyses representing that diversity which is, however, united by ethnographic method (more on this issue see e.g. Buchowski 2019).

a part of humanness and its particularity rooted in cultural and historical circumstances seem to provide a conducive prism for anthropological inquiry (see Ortner 2006: 129–153). However, such an approach is being commonly shaped by unproblematized premises of critical humanism that relates to "symbolic interactionism, pragmatism, democratic thinking, storytelling, moral progress, redistribution, justice and good citizenship," and privileges "experience, meaning, and human subjectivity" (Plummer 2005: 359, 370). Those presumptions have therefore been denaturalized mainly due to critiques originating from the post-structural thought. Rosalind Morris (2007: 360–361) points out that Ortner's call "for a recognition of the intentionality, subjectivity, and agency of individual actors ..., who '(try to) act on the world even as they are acted upon' (Ortner 2006: 110)" should be analyzed with regard to its links with neohumanist "possessive individualism." On the other hand, thus understood agency reflects, in a sense, commodity logic that brings a concept of personhood defined by discrete attributes and boundaries, whereas "society" and "the individual" are seen as mutually forming antinomies, situated in specific relations of power (more on this issue see Strathern 1990: 3–40).

The above problems do not need, however, to limit analytical potential of a notion of agency. They just require that the above idea of personhood and the specific vision of human acting subjects rooted in critical humanism become unsettled and removed from its very center. Following Tom Boellstorf's (2007) discussion of a problematic relationship between concepts of gender and sexuality, one can think about agency not in semantic terms, that is, what it means, but in the pragmatic ones, that is, what it does. This, in turn, allows for asking how agency works for producing, sustaining, and destabilizing the social, which can all be recognized ethnographically. Such an approach seems particularly vital for ethnographies in/of late industrialism. Kim Fortun (2012: 451–452, 453) defines "late industrial times" as "complex conditions, conditions involving many nested systems – technical, biophysical, cultural, economic – and thus a multiplicity of interactions, which keep the parameters of 'the problem' from ever settling down." This complexity brings uncertainty related to "discursive gaps," when there is "no way of thinking that can grasp what is at hand," and "discursive risks," which result in "a tendency to rely on established idioms and ways of thinking, nonetheless." Facing late industrialism, ethnography needs therefore to work as an experimental system "that generates surprises" and remains "open to intervention and foreigners." Looking at agency through this prism allows to grasp how social phenomena of late industrial world are emerging at the intersections of diverse processes of various scales (see Rabinow et al. 2008: 74–81).

The discussed theoretical premises have all in one way or another shaped the team research project entitled *Conflict, Tension and Cooperation: A Case Study of Mutual Impact between the Opole Power Plant and the Community of Dobrzeń Wielki*,[3] which comprised the point of departure of this book. Its purpose was to explore and analyze multidimensional and interrelated cultural, social, political, and economic processes of late industrialism, which were both the result and the context of interactions between the Opole Power Plant (OPP) and the community of Dobrzeń Wielki commune in Opole Silesia in southwestern Poland. Initially, the project took as its focus the expansion of the OPP conducted between 2014 and 2019, which at that time was one of the largest industrial investments in energy sector in Europe. However, the plan of shifting administrative borders of the neighboring city of Opole (including a takeover of the part of Dobrzeń Wielki commune's territory with the OPP) announced in late 2015, and put in force on January 1, 2017, has also importantly shaped the research situation. In the above circumstances, the project aimed at developing analytical frameworks for exploring the complex interplay between a local community and an industrial investment; at enhancing theoretical and practical understanding of conflicts, tensions and cooperation which emerge at the intersections of interests embedded in specific local, national, European and global scales; and at deepening scientific understanding of discourses and practices within the context of ambiguities resulting from the accelerated change. To this end, between

3 The project was implemented from August 2014 to January 2019 at the University of Wroclaw with Petr Skalník as the Principal Investigator, and financed by the National Science Center, grant number 2013/11/b/HS3/03895.

2015 and 2018 the research team of scholars based in two Polish universities, the University of Wroclaw and the Jagiellonian University in Cracow, conducted intensive, ethnographic field research focused on five overlapping research areas: politics, economics, ethnic and inter-group relations, gender relations, and migration and mobility. Some of their findings have been already published (see e.g. Skalník 2018). Others constitute a topic of this book.

The edited collection entitled *Agency at Work: Ethnographies in/of Late Industrialism* brought together analyses rooted in both ethnological and anthropological traditions materialized through an ethnographic detail. Whereas every chapter discusses issues related to the project main research areas, they are all engaged in conversations with one another, revealing various forms of agency in the specifically situated late industrial settings. In the opening chapter, Petr Skalník investigates the agency of the OPP as an important sociopolitical catalyzer of events in the Dobrzeń Wielki commune, both in a historical perspective and with regard to its recent expansion. In this context, he presents the process of initiating a construction of the OPP back in the 1970s; the changing relationships between the OPP and the community of the Dobrzeń Wielki commune from the mid-1990s, when the first four blocks of the plant started to operate; the political circumstances which brought a decision to enlarge the OPP with two more blocks; and further developments related to the ongoing expansion and the commune's administrative division. These detailed analysis of "the most important political moments" related to the OPP has been located in a wider frame of discussion on energy security and (de)carbonization in the age of global overheating (Eriksen 2016). Thus, this is not only the OPP but also the European Union and the Polish nation state which are shown as important political agents molding the researched events in the Dobrzeń Wielki commune.

In the next chapter, Konrad Górny also analyzes contemporary phenomena with a view to a broader historical frame. His main analytical focus comprises a local community understood not in a traditional way, as a "comprehensive social structure" characterized by social cohesion, but as an entity "open to changes" rooted in "the local government community model." In this context, the author shows how due to industrialization process the specific community of Dobrzeń Wielki commune has been changing, mostly in socio-economic terms, since the late nineteenth century until today. Against this background, Górny ponders over the OPP enlargement and the commune's administrative division taken as entanglements of various scales. In particular, he is interested in dynamics of economic transformation, and its potential to shape local community. While for many years the Dobrzeń Wielki commune had been successfully developing, the takeover of the OPP and other large companies by the city of Opole made its future uncertain. Seeing the presented analysis, the fate of local community would not solely be determined by lost revenues, but first of all, by a lost sense of agency.

The chapter by Mirosław Marczyk sheds more light on the above issues. The author provides a detailed account of bottom-up activities undertaken by Dobrzeń Wielki commune's residents as a response to the OPP enlargement. In this context, a specific attention is given to the intersections of economic, political, and cultural dimensions of the studied forms of agency. The discussed economic strategies are differentiated both in view of specific branches and a size of businesses. Small entrepreneurs have mainly engaged, with different outcomes, in services and trade. In contrast, large companies have managed to win a couple of contracts related to the construction of new blocks of the power plant. In both cases, however, the OPP expansion has not provided sufficient (and expected) revenues. However, while the small entrepreneurship has at times been facing bankruptcy, the large one used this situation as a trigger for moving their activities to the supra-local markets. The economic strategies of local subjects immersed in the late industrial world thus demonstrate that in one way or another, a big industrial investment activates complex connections extending far beyond its actual sitting.

In contrast, Marcin Brocki takes up an issue of ethnic divisions in the Dobrzeń Wielki commune, which were revived by a political dispute over changing commune's administrative borders. This, in turn, generated a social and political crisis spreading outside this particular locality. In his analysis the author shows how an ethnically diverse local community has responded to a politically inspired attack aimed to justify and reinforce the national government's right to decide on local issues. Deprived of agency by the subsequent nation states in *longue durée* sense, the local community has historically formed a specific "local identity." Facing such deprivation again, it refused to fit into the national government's narrative on ethnic disparities, and developed instead a certain unity, which allowed residents to actively engage in a social protest. Although ethnicity has not ceased to play an important role in everyday life of the commune, the discussed crisis endowed people with new signs of identity rooted in the memory of common struggle. A newly acquired sense of agency thus enriched the local semiosphere with symbolic resources of integration above ethnic divisions.

The next chapter also puts the Dobrzeń Wielki commune's administrative division in its very center. In her analysis, Monika Baer focuses on agency of emotions which produced affective togetherness in the field of the political that emerged in a response to the above circumstances. Its actual forms have been, however, changing over time, bringing not only the common social protest discussed by Brocki but also critical communicative performances within the protesting commune. In this context, the author gives a special attention to Arjun Appadurai's (2013: 295) "ethics of probability" and "ethics of possibility" by the use of which the commune's residents tried to anticipate an uncertain future. While the former embodied fears connected to the planned division, the latter expressed hope for a "good life." However, when the anticipated takeover of the part of the commune became the daily present, the shape of "possible" has evolved. This, in turn, has reconfigured the affective togetherness, shifted poles of the field of the political, and redefined the local scene of politics. The discussed workings of emotions thus demonstrate that affective dimensions constitute an important, though frequently overlooked, aspect of every political event.

Unlike the above-mentioned chapters, the one by Ewa Kruk focuses on the site of OPP expansion per se. The author investigates gendered divisions in the construction consortium with a special attention given to (re)constructing femininity staged by women employed by companies building up the OPP new blocks. To this purpose, she analyzes how specific interactions and phenomena experienced by women working in a men-dominated workplace have been shaping their ideas about gender and their strategic uses (and abuses) in negotiating their own positioning in that environment. By "doing" and "undoing" femininity, the interlocutors aimed to minimize "gender-related inconveniences." On the one hand, their attempts to become "one of the boys" involved adopting male-style behavior and disregard for conventional forms of femininity. On the other one, "small and subtle acts of resistance" allowed them to subvert the actual lack of construction site's most valuable symbolic capital – masculinity. The discussed gendered agency thus reveals dynamic, flexible, processual, discontinuous, but also accidental dimensions of (un)doing gender in the context of industrial investment.

Last but not least, in the final chapter Marek Pawlak ponders over another aspect of the construction site of the OPP new blocks, namely the mobile livelihoods of construction workers exemplified by residents of a worker's hostel situated next to the power plant. To this end, he explores strategies of negotiating spatial and temporal arrangements resulting from temporary work contracts and characteristics of the industrial site. In this context, the author shows how the wider entanglements of late industrialism and its specificity embodied by industrial work- and dwelling places have been all materialized in affective attunements performed by the workers in question. The temporariness of "being there" generates flexibility and indifference toward constantly changing visited localities. At the same time, mobile livelihoods bring also ambiguous feelings toward these places which should feel "like home" – places of residence. Against this background, Pawlak attempts to problematize a concept of agency as "a form of affective dealings with encountered predicaments." Thus, understood agency proves to be a useable tool to muddle through neoliberal and late industrial condition.

The discussed chapters demonstrate ethnographically how agency may work to create, reinforce, and unsettle various dimensions of the social in specifically localized settings of late industrial world seen as effects of variables and forces of various scales. The investigated topics deals with phenomena seemingly related to a single commune of Dobrzeń Wielki. Still, they shed some light on processes constitutive for the regional, national, European, or even global contemporary understood as "a moving image of modernity, moving through the recent past and near future," yet also defined by a "grid of connections" which are not purely mental, and "vectors of power and force lines" that cannot be controlled (Rabinow et al., 2008: 58, 77). More importantly, the applied analytical perspectives go in many ways beyond limitations of critical humanism with its specific vision of personhood and human acting subjects. By focusing on the OPP, interactions between the local community and wider economic transformations, entrepreneurship, the uniting semiosphere of the ethnically divided local group, workings of emotions in the field of the political, (un)doing gender in the industrial workplace, or mobile livelihoods, all authors in one way or another attempts to escape problems raised by conventional idea of agency that puts intentional human subjects in its center. On the other hand, these analyses have obviously been attainable thanks to actual people living in particular time and place (Abu-Lughod 1991: 153). This is them who really made this book possible. By way of conclusion, we would like therefore to express our deep gratitude to all residents of Dobrzeń Wielki commune and neighboring areas, employees of the OPP and construction consortium as well as scholars and officials based in Opole for their willingness to share their time, experience and stories with us.

References

Abu-Lughod, Lila. "Writing against Culture." In: *Recapturing Anthropology: Working in the Present*, ed. Richard G. Fox. Santa Fe: School of American Research Press, 1991, pp. 137–162.

Appadurai, Arjun. *The Future as Cultural Fact: Essays on the Global Condition*. London: Verso, 2013.

Barth, Fredrik and Andre Gingrich, Robert Parkin, Sydel Silverman. *One Discipline, Four Ways: British, German, French, and American Anthropology*. Chicago: The University of Chicago Press, 2005.

Boellstorff, Tom. "Queer Studies in the House of Anthropology." *Annual Review of Anthropology* 36/2007, pp. 17–35.

Buchowski, Michał ed. *Twilight Zone Anthropology: Voices from Poland*. Herefordshire: Sean Kingston Publishing, 2019.

Eriksen, Thomas Hylland. *Overheating: An Anthropology of Accelerated Change*. London: Pluto Press, 2016.

Fortun, Kim. "Ethnography in Late Industrialism." *Cultural* Anthropology 27(3)/2012. pp. 446–464.

Morris, Rosalind C. "Legacies of Derrida: Anthropology." *Annual Review of Anthropology* 36/2007, pp. 355–389.

Ortner, Sherry B. "Theory in Anthropology since the Sixties." *Comparative Studies in Society and* History 26(1)/1984, pp. 126–166.

Ortner, Sherry B. *Anthropology and Social Theory: Culture, Power, and the Acting Subject*. Durham: Duke University Press, 2006.

Plummer, Ken. "Critical Humanism and Queer Theory: Living with the Tensions." In: *The Sage Handbook of Qualitative Research: Third Edition*, Norman K. Denzin and Yvonna S. Lincoln. Thousand Oaks: Sage, 2005, pp. 357–373.

Rabinow, Paul and George E. Marcus. James D. Faubion, Tobias Rees. *Designs for an Anthropology of the Contemporary*, Durham: Duke University Press, 2008.

Skalník, Petr ed. *Mutual Impact: Conflict, Tension and Cooperation in Opole Silesia*. Wrocław: Uniwersytet Wrocławski, 2018.

Strathern, Marilyn. *The Gender of the Gift: Problems with Women and Problems with Society in Melanesia*. Berkeley: University of California Press, 1990.

Petr Skalník[1]

Opole Power Plant as a Sociopolitical Catalyzer

Abstract: This introductory chapter deals with the coal as energy security and tackles the agency of Dobrzeń Wielki commune vis-à-vis Opole Power Plant and its expansion while a local self-government faces takeover of the part of commune's administrative territory by the neighboring city of Opole. These events are being discussed in a wider context of divergent energy policies endorsed by the European Union and the Polish nation state, respectively.

Keywords: coal, Dobrzeń Wielki, energy security, local self-government, Opole.

Energy Security and Decarbonization

Energy security appears as one of the decisive factors in keeping the human civilization in balance. On the one hand, most of 200 nation states and territories would like to be autarkic energetically, on the other, they realize that it is virtually impossible. Not every country is rich in energy resources and thus is compelled to seek these resources abroad by way of trade or territorial annexation. Those energetically rich sell their surplus in energy to other countries. Some wars, both historically distant and recent, were fought over energy resources. It can be argued that future wars are to be fought in direct dependence on the demand for energy resources. Even without energy wars the unequal distribution of energy resources will lead to regional and global tensions.

Globalization has brought about an ever-increasing realization that energy resources should be treated with economic cautiousness, especially those deemed exhaustible such as fossil fuels. Viewing the limited supply of these fuels, some countries have embarked on gaining energy from nuclear fuel and the most advanced even rejected nuclear energy in favor

1 Associate Professor Emeritus, University of Wroclaw, skalnik.petr@gmail.com.

of renewable energy resources such as wind, sun, and water. This shift is justified ideologically by pointing out to general overheating (Eriksen 2016) or rising average temperatures called global heating, especially in some particular localities on the globe (cf. Eriksen 2018). Recently, gas and oil are gained from cracking shale rocks, which also raises worries about human intervention because explosives and chemicals are used in fracking.

Worldwide and within particular countries debates are raging as to whether the measurable increase in average temperature is part of global climate change caused by human activities or rather, we are witnessing only a temporary change irrespective of human civilization. Theoreticians have come up with the concept of Anthropocene, a new kind of geological period principally determined by human energy consumption (Hauhs et al. 2017). Since the early twenty-first century, the above issues have also become a center of significant number of studies in social sciences, including social and cultural anthropology. Researchers have been analyzing social, cultural, and ecological impact of late industrial investments. Within this genre, it was stressed that major industrial installations have been closely related to nuclear tragedies of Chernobyl and Fukushima (Fujikawa 2015; Gill 2014; Hasegawa 2014; Inose 2014) or the tragic explosion in chemical works of Bhopal (Fortun 2001). However, also impacts of projects which did not explode were scrutinized. Such are cases of Bhilai Steel Works in India (Parry 2015), Austrian built coal power station such as that in northern Turkey (Knudsen 2015) or hydroelectric power stations and dams such as Three Gorges in China (Wallace 2019). In this context, studies of mining projects, such as Panguna, Ok Tedi or Lihir in Papua New Guinea (Filer 2012) or fracking in Australia and other parts of the world were carried out. The rights of the local populations have been infringed upon, land grabs took place in connection with these projects, while protests and armed struggle led to the closure of some of them (De Rijke 2013; Trigger et al. 2014; Eriksen 2018).

Coal Controversy in the European Union and Poland

In the European Union (EU) coal power generation reaches 24 percent of all power generation at the moment. The main producers of coal and lignite and their consumers for power generation purposes are Germany and Poland. In Poland, for example the bituminous coal burning Opole Power Plant (OPP) was recently expanded to more than double capacity of 3342 MW. This is against the EU policy of decarbonization (Dupont, Oberthür 2015). As far as Poland is concerned, it has the largest lignite powered station in the world, situated in Bełchatów in central Poland with installed energy output 5472 MW. This power plant was alternatively called the biggest carbon polluter in the EU, the largest carbon dioxide emitter (34.9 million ton per annum, in 2016), and the most climate damaging power plant in the EU. Before expansion, OPP had installed output 1532 MW and emitted "only" 5.82 million ton of carbon dioxide per annum. That was despite installed modern filters. At present, after the expansion, OPP will rank among the biggest European bituminous coal powered stations. While the former Polish government (established by the Civic Platform political party) paid some attention to the EU policy of phasing-out coal, the present one (appointed by the Law and Justice political party after winning the election in 2015) made clear that the importance of domestic coal will remain high.

Lignite consumption in the EU reached 58.3 percent of EU's coal consumption. The EU started its decarbonization policy at the beginning of the new millennium. In 2008 emission trading system was launched. However, in the years 2010–2012 coal power generation increased in the EU being called "Coal Renaissance." New coal power plants were put to operation in Germany, Italy, the Netherlands, and Poland beside other countries of Eastern Europe. According to Yoko Ito (2017: 8), "Poland is the largest steam coal producer in the EU, and coal's share in the generation mix is as high as more than 80 %." At the same time, power demand is expected to grow while energy security vis-à-vis volatility of gas supply from Russia is a top priority for Poland. Thus, reliance on coal as energy supplier even increases.

According to European Commission, by 2030 the power mix of Poland will change substantially including 65 percent of coal, 14.9 percent of gas, and 18.5 percent of renewable energy (Ito 2017: 10). In line with this goal, coal will remain strategically decisive for the energy independence of the country. The country, though paying lip-service to the phasing-out policy of the EU, is not going to substantially change its dependence on coal for power generation. Critics such as Remigiusz Rosicki (2015: 58, 54) point out that "[i]n the long run, the national electricity system will still be based on coal mining," but at the same time assert that "the Polish state is not interested in the modernization processes of the energy sector, which gives the advantage to the conventional energy suppliers," and lament the "poor condition of the Polish coal mining sector." According to Ito (2017: 14), "Poland has a serious concern in energy security and domestic coal industry protection, thus no plausible path has been seen for reducing coal power generation substantially." The draft of Energy Policy of Poland till 2050 "envisages the continuation of the objectives laid down in 2009, which *per se* leaves no illusions as to any possible revolution in the energy sector in Poland," meaning at the same time "minimalistic approach to the observance of the EU requirements in the area of RES" (Rosicki 2015: 55–56).

The Polish energy policy document of 2009 delineating the aims of the country until 2030 is still valid, although the above-mentioned 2050 draft was published in August 2014. It should have been widely discussed but thus far no final word was said, which may be connected with the coming to power of the new Law and Justice government before the end of 2015. While the policy until 2030 respects to some extent the tenets of the EU, the 2050 document has come with three different strategies to be discussed by specialists: balanced, nuclear, and gas plus renewable sources (RES). According to the balanced scenario, coal and lignite will remain main sources of energy generation but 15 percent of generation will be assured by two nuclear power plants, while the role of gas and RES will also reach up to 20 percent. The nuclear scenario accounts for 45–60 percent of energy from nuclear power plants, and only 10–15 percent from coal power plants. The share of oil and gas will each be 10–15 percent while RES – 15 percent. Finally the scenario gas plus RES projects 50–55 percent of gas and RES (from it 20 percent of gas RES), 30 percent of coal, 15–20 percent of oil and 10 percent of nuclear energy (Projekt 2015).

In 2020, however, Poland accepted the EU strategy of reduction carbon dioxide by 2050.

The Opole Power Plant

Viewing these economic, political, and social ramifications, the construction of fifth and sixth blocks of the OPP fits well into the Polish national strategies. What is, however, puzzling is the location of the OPP within Poland, the means by which coal is to be conveyed to it, and the relation between Dobrzeń Wielki as a self-governing commune and the neighboring urban commune of Opole. The location of the OPP is a result of complex deliberations which started already during the Second World War. The site was selected out of several candidates and according to all informants[2] the criteria were geographical and economic. At the time of the decision there was no particular political reason why the OPP should stand where it is today. Between 1954–1972, the original building site belonged to the Czarnowąsy *Gromada* (the lowest tier of local government in the Polish People's Republic) that preceded the Czarnowąsy commune. The latter was fused with the Dobrzeń Wielki commune established in January1973.

The role of the Odra River was considered as the construction plot is in short distance from it. Indeed, the original idea was to transport the bituminous coal from the Upper Silesian Coal Basin via the Gliwice Canal and the Odra River, to build a special port in the vicinity of the building plot and to transport coal to the power station via a conveyor system. This plan was abandoned during the construction of the OPP that took approximately 20 years (from the mid-1970s until the mid-1990s). Railways as the coal transporter took preference when a direct railway line was built to the site.

2 My fieldwork was carried out in different stages of the research project *Conflict, tension and cooperation* between 2015 and 2018. I had circa 80 formal and informal interviews plus casual chats with dozens of Dobrzeń Wielki commune's inhabitants, a number of formal interviews with important Opole officials, the Mayor of Opole included. I also talked to a handful of locally based academics, including those working at the University of Opole and the Silesian Institute in Opole.

In spite of steady promotion of the Odra River as the ideal, economic and ecological, avenue for transport of coal to OPP, Ryszard Galla, repeatedly elected to the Polish parliament as an MP for the German minority, and others were not successful. Galla succeeded in establishing the Group of Friends of Odra in the Polish parliament. He arranged a special exhibition on the history of Odra navigability. However, he is otherwise fairly skeptical as to reaching the grade 3 or 4 of Odra navigability. The problem consists in the many years of neglect. However, he believes that if Odra is made navigable as far as Ostrava on the Czech side, there will be lot of interest in the Czech Republic to use Odra as an important transport route to the sea. What is however also necessary is to build the sluice at Malczyce near Wrocław. The turbines were supplied by a Czech company, but these were not installed, and penalty had to be paid for that.[3] The enlargement of OPP with blocks fifth and sixth does not count with the Odra River and further plans are to use railways. The letter of intention on navigability of Odra signed by several personalities with great fanfare during the Self-government Congress at Opole on October 17, 2016, has to my mind only a symbolic value because no concrete implementation measures have thus far been taken and the costs seem to be astronomical. The pertinent minister limits himself to repeating that there has been urgency in creating the Odra Riverway Administration, but it seems that there is not enough political will to start real work on the project. Besides, one must consider the powerful coal-railway lobby used to make profits by bringing coal to the OPP for the last three decades.

The Dobrzeń Wielki Commune

The territory of the commune was chosen for the construction of OPP by default. There seems to have been no say by this commune as to the placement of the power plant. The inhabitants of the previously existing Czarnowąsy commune were practically compelled to sign contracts on sale of their plots to the state (represented by the management of OPP) and as far as memory goes, original reactions of residents of the Dobrzeń Wielki commune to the construction was negative. The inhabitants of

3 An interview with Galla conducted on August 12, 2015.

nearby Opole were also reported as opposed to the construction. No document was found which would mention any conflict about OPP between the commune of Opole and the commune of Dobrzeń Wielki. Apparently, the power of the communist state was such that nobody really dared to officially express opposition to OPP and its parameters.

In the early 1970s works on a major coal power station, called OPP, started. The location was one of the proposed placings that had been situated along the Odra River, a waterway serving for centuries as an artery of Silesia. Although originally six blocks were planned, only four were put to operation by 1993–1997. A special housing estate emerged gradually next to Dobrzeń Wielki village to house the external workers on OPP. Locals also found work in OPP. The first block was launched in 1993. Fortunately, OPP was provided with most advanced desulphuring filters which made it one of the state-of-the-art power plants, less polluting its environs. Thus, the local population gradually adjusted to the existence of a giant power plant on the territory of the commune. They as well adjusted to the new neighbors in the housing estate "Energetyk."

When I first arrived in the Dobrzeń Wielki commune in 2005, I was expecting to carry out a re-study of ethnic relations and general social change but did not know that there was a major power plant there (Skalník 2004, 2005, 2008). The previous sociological studies were aimed at ethnicity and industrialization (Ossowski 1947; Nowakowski 1960; Olszewska 1969). Therefore, subsequent research of 2006–2007, which also involved short fieldtrips by students from the University of Pardubice (the Czech Republic) and the University of Wrocław (Poland), was not particularly aimed at studying OPP, but various aspects of life in Dobrzeń Wielki villages. An exception was an extensive BA thesis by Tomáš Sabela (University of Pardubice), who studied social aspects of entrepreneurship in the commune (Sabela 2008).

One of the results of the first phase of the research was that ethnicity did not play an active role in the life of inhabitants of the Dobrzeń Wielki commune. Moreover, OPP was a kind of neutral player in the social fabric of the area (Skalník 2007). Meanwhile, by 2007 OPP became part of the Polish Energy Group (PGE) with the seat in Belchatów in central Poland. After 2010 I continued to carry out summer fieldwork practice in Dobrzeń Wielki with my Wroclaw students. During our repeated stays we learned about the revival, on a higher level of sophistication, of the original plans of construction of the fifth and sixth blocks of OPP. These two blocks were to be the mightiest single investment in the history of modern Poland. They were to be more powerful than all four existing blocks together and their construction would have to be completed within mere five years, which contrasts with more than 20 years for the original power station. Up to 3000 workers at a time were to carry out the construction.

Once the project was made public, a controversy emerged. The PGE was more concerned about its shareholders' wellbeing than Poland's increasing need for electric energy. For a while it looked as if the expansion of OPP would be postponed. The construction of the fifth and sixth blocks of OPP became an important political issue. The Opole voivodeship as the smallest region in Poland needed badly an important investment that would enhance the economic and thus also political position of the region within the country. Otherwise, it was feared that the region might be divided and added to the neighboring regions of Lower and Upper Silesia. Especially Opole politicians and local patriotic public were trying to prove that OPP must be expanded for the sake of development of the region and stave off the exodus of population from it. Our preliminary surveys carried out in 2012, 2013 and 2014 showed that the inhabitants of the Dobrzeń Wielki commune had no objections against the construction, but they were not engaged in any political struggle. Eventually the Polish government of Donald Tusk (Civic Platform), representing the Polish state, which is the main shareholder of PGE, decided in June 2014 that indeed the expansion of OPP would start soon.

The above events formed the starting point of the team research projects entitled *Conflict, Tension and Cooperation: A Case Study of Mutual Impact between the Opole Power Plant and the Community of Dobrzeń Wielki* conducted between August 2014 and January 2019.[4] It began approximately at the same time as the construction of the fifth and sixth blocks of the OPP was launched. The first short field trip by the whole project team took place in February 2015 and was followed by individual

---

4 The project was implemented at the University of Wroclaw with me as the Principal Investigator. It was financed by the National Science Center (NSC), grant number 2013/11/b/HS3/03895.

team members' fieldwork research in next years. The previously established contacts within the commune of Dobrzeń Wielki and with Opole academics[5] were now expanded to include the leadership of OPP and the construction consortium responsible for the OPP's enlargement. One of the findings during the first phase of this research was that very few residents of Dobrzeń Wielki commune were hired to join the consortium although many were promised jobs by the then vice-mayor of the village of Brzezie (because of that failure he was recalled from his post). Furthermore, very few formal contacts between the construction consortium and the leadership of Dobrzeń Wielki were established because the consortium functioned as a closed community whose members spent weekends away from the commune. It is called "Chinese technique" when the investor brings along their own workers who do not mingle with the local population.

From "Giełczyn" to Dobrzeń Wielki

Until 2016 Dobrzeń Wielki was a fairly large commune in the Opole voivodeship of Upper Silesia consisting of nine villages. The area was under Prussian/German rule for two hundred years until 1945. In the wake of Second World War local Silesian population was not expelled to Germany like in other countries such as Czechoslovakia, even though many local Silesians were Germanized and did not feel Polish. Dobrzeń Wielki (under the pseudonym of Giełczyn) was studied in 1945–1946 by Stanisław Ossowski, a well-known Polish sociologist, who was interested in ethnic relations there, both historically (in a context of plebiscite of 1921) and at the moment of research when ethnic Poles, expelled from eastern borderlands of Poland annexed to the Soviet Union, were resettled in Silesia (Ossowski 1947; cf. Czech 2015). Later the village of Dobrzeń Wielki (not the whole commune) was studied by rural sociologists such as Stefan Nowakowski (1960) and Anna Olszewska (1969). They were interested in social change, especially in the industrialization of Dobrzeń

5 They were involved in preparations for a major research project during the spring of 2013. When it appeared to be too complex and thus hardly manageable, a smaller seven-member research team of scholars from Wroclaw and Cracow was formed and applied for a more modest, though still ambitious project which received funding from NSC.

Wielki. In 1973 the state decided to form the Dobrzeń Wielki commune from 9 villages around that village (Dobrzeń Wielki, Chróścice, Dobrzeń Mały, Borki, Świerkle, Brzezie, Czarnowąsy, Krzanowice, and Kup). During the communist rule (1945–1989) German language was suppressed and Polonization was carried out. Since 1990 German national minority was recognized by the state and those who declared that they belonged to it could obtain German passports along with Polish citizenship. That made possible labor migration to Germany and subsequent affluence of the villagers, but also outmigration of the young people.

Pękala

In 1979, Józef Pękala was appointed the third director of the state enterprise OPP in construction. He was to remain on his post for more than 20 years. He had previous experience as a director of two other power plants in the area where three former powers, Russia, Austria and Prussia touched borders. Himself originating from the Polish East, Pękala had to acquaint himself with mentalities that dominated the area. When we met for two formal interviews, he stressed that especially Silesian central values, the family, women, and the dialect, sharply contrasted with Polish values of patriotism. The Silesian homeland (in German *Heimat*) is something genuine Poles do not know, for them it is motherland or the state that must be defended, but homeland stands in the way of that. Without taking sides, Pękala's principle was sensitiveness to the local values.[6] He mentioned the case of a local man whose house was to be destroyed so that OPP could be built. Pękala received the man, listened attentively to his complaint and promised a redress. Risking problems with his superiors, he managed to get building material for a substitute house and made sure that the house was built. Another case was when he defended his opinion that there was no need to fence the building site because he was sure that nobody would steal anything from the open-air storage. Again, he relied on his reading of the character of Silesians. Of course, when the building was close to completion the fence was built for security reasons.

6 Interviews were conducted on October 31, 2015, and April 3, 2016.

In his contribution that was placed as a preface into the first volume on the socio-economic transformations caused in the Dobrzeń Wielki commune by OPP (an outcome of the first conference on these issues), Pękala (1988: 5) stressed that

> we have to care more for coexistence of the arrivals with the local people. Our primary goal is to create harmonious relations between the operational staff, the builders of the power plant and the inhabitants of the neighboring settlements. It means to preserve all positive traits of that environment and care so that these traits are transferred to the soil of the collective of the power plant. It is as well to care so that the staff of the power plant learns and accepts the whole history of the region, somewhat inherits and continues it.

He put these ideas to life. He regularly met with Alojzy Kokot, the long-term head of the Dobrzeń Wielki commune, with whom he built a good personal relationship. Kokot not once mentioned that in his conversations with me. He himself in his paper presented in the same volume stressed that those who moved into commune because of the construction of OPP were not interested in the social life in the commune, with the exception of religion. He was not in favor of mass immigration so that there was a "chance to save local culture and custom. One needs to admit that the leadership of the power plant and also designers of the housing estate are in favor of this moderate integration of the immigrants and local community" (Kokot 1988: 162). With the support of OPP and its director, several conferences followed that of 1988 and publications came out that map the relationship between the Dobrzeń Wielki commune and the OPP.

Sociological Research

A considerable attention among Opole sociologists was paid to the question of relations between the population of Dobrzeń Wielki commune and the OPP. Besides the above-mentioned collection of essays published in 1988 (that is, during the last year before the Round Table negotiations and the end of communist power monopoly in Poland), there were three other collective works published that discussed various aspects of OPP (Łuszczewska 1993; Lesiuk et al. 2000; Rosik-Dulewska, Kusz 2009). All of them were subsidized by the OPP, while the involvement of the Silesian Institute in Opole (with which most of the Opole sociologists were related) was not negligible in the studies and publication.[7] The question is about the quality of research, its ratio between quantitative and qualitative approach. Not all these articles belong to social sciences, some are contributions from the natural sciences. What is, however, sure is that most of these texts were not based on prolonged stay and direct daily contacts with the inhabitants of the Dobrzeń Wielki commune. The approach from social and cultural anthropology, which underlay research in the project *Conflict, tension and cooperation*, is basically qualitative, based on participant observation, interviews, sometimes even observing participation (e.g. living in the dormitory together with workers employed in OPP or its expansion). I do not want to say that anthropological approach is better, but will stress that it is a legitimate method that thus far was not tested on the issue of the relationship between Dobrzeń Wielki commune and OPP. It is, however, intriguing that in the four above-mentioned books there are hardly papers that would pertain to the relationship of the mutual impact type. Most of them discuss various aspect of the impact of OPP on the Dobrzeń Wielki commune, but hardly the other way around. That would mean that the commune has had no or little impact on OPP, which is impossible. One of the early researchers working in the Silesian Institute was the late Ryszard Kałuża, whose residence was in the commune. This researcher cared for a sensitive approach so that OPP "did not destroy positive family, neighbor, religious and labor ties in the local society" (Kałuża 1988: 10). He continuously followed the changes until his untimely death in 2009.

The Relationship between the OPP and the Dobrzeń Wielki Commune

The conducted research showed that in the beginning both populations of the Dobrzeń Wielki commune and of the city of Opole were not in favor of the construction of OPP. However, as time passed and the

7 Teresa Sołdra-Gwiżdż (2009: 47) mentioned that an agreement between the OPP director Józef Pękala and an interdisciplinary research team under the leadership of Robert Rauziński, based in the Silesian Institute, was reached in 1984 about a continuous monitoring of past and present situation in Dobrzeń Wielki during the construction and exploitation of the OPP.

coordination of activities between the leadership of OPP and the leadership of the commune intensified, residents not only got used to the existence of the construction site and the presence of numerous construction workers but started to evaluate positively these new features. Some of the commune inhabitants were able to get work as employees of OPP. The attitudes toward the housing estate "Energetyk" also changed from resentment to acceptance. Eventually much later some well-to-do residents of "Energetyk" sold their apartments and built new family houses on several streets of Dobrzeń Wielki proper. Once the OPP was put to exploitation in the years 1993–97, the modern filters were mounted on the exhausts of OPP which made it even more acceptable if not welcome by the inhabitants of villages within the commune. Therefore, based on this positive experience, there was hardly any voice uttered against the expansion of OPP by blocks fifth and sixth when the Wroclaw students interviewed the inhabitants in 2011–2014. The Dobrzeń Wielki commune received a substantial sum yearly as tax on land and enterprises on it. From the proceeds the commune could finance various development projects. One of the largest such projects was a park symbolically connecting the center of Dobrzeń Wielki with the housing estate "Energetyk." Dobrzeń Wielki commune has become one of the most prosperous communes in Poland. Politically these successes have been ascribed to the "German minority" that continuously won the local government election for at least four consecutive four-year periods until 2014.

Struggle for a Decision

The final decision of the Polish government to start the construction of fifth and sixth blocks was reached without lobbying by the leadership and population of the Dobrzeń Wielki commune. It was Solidarity trade union at OPP, Opole journalists and some regional politicians who reacted strongly against the reluctance of the directors of PGE in Bełchatów to decide in favor of the construction. As written above, the OPP was incorporated into the new PGE in 2007, and in 2009 the leadership of PGE decided to proceed with the expansion of the OPP by the two originally planned blocks five and six. But these would not be blocks identical with the other already installed four blocks, each of capacity 360 MW. Each new block would have capacity 900 MW which means that the two new blocks would supersede the capacity of the existing four blocks. After that initial decision the old original foundations of block five and six were removed so that the newly conceived blocks could be constructed there. Although the project work was commissioned and drawings with documentation performed, there was no final decision taken as to when the construction should begin. Meanwhile also the tender for the construction consortium took place in 2011 and the winner was the one including Rafako SA, Polimex-Mostostal SA and Mostostal Warszawa SA. After some necessary legal and financial steps were taken and the leadership of PGE was expected to begin the construction proper, its CEO Krzysztof Kilian announced on April 4, 2013 that the PGE would not proceed with the construction of blocks five and six because the company calculated that it would not be profitable and that was not in the interest of the shareholders. One should remind the reader that by far the main shareholder in the PGE is the Polish state. The following day, the Polish Prime Minister Tusk said at a press conference that although the PGE was a stock exchange company and may have its calculations of loss and profit, however the state had its shares in the PGE and the vital interests of the state had to be respected. He said that there was only one interest and that was cheap energy for the Polish people, from which both the company and the Polish state would profit.

In Opole and in OPP initiatives were created that demanded explanation and that the decision of PGE leadership should be rescinded. A special press conference organized by the trade union Solidarity and Sławomir Kłosowski, the MP for the then opposition party Law and Justice, took place on April 9, 2013 and a resolution was approved calling the administration of PGE and the government to proceed with the construction. The whole matter became a political affair. On May 27 a special meeting was organized at OPP, which accepted an action program "Yes to Power Plant – Yes to Silesia." A petition was sent to the President, Prime Minister and Minister of Economy, and it was decided about a picketing action in front of the Voivodeship Office in Opole. Moreover, a tent township would be erected in Czarnowąsy where signatures would be collected under the appeal calling for the construction. Meanwhile the consultative body of the Office of the President "Energy Security" met, where Prime Minister

Tusk declared that the expansion of OPP was one of the many investments which the Civic Platform government promised to realize. After a thorough analysis of all the market data the government would find means and ways so that this investment would be carried out in accordance with the intentions. This gave hope that the expansion of OPP would eventually occur. Nevertheless, the picketing took place on June 7, but the voivode hesitated to give support. The tent township in Czarnowąsy managed to stop or delay transport on 454 regional road between Opole and Dobrzeń Wielki that also leads to OPP. On June 8 the MPs of the then oppositional party Law and Justices (Mariusz Błaszczak, Wojciech Jasiński, Grzegorz Tobiszowski, and above-mentioned Kłosowski) visited tent township and supported the protesters. Błaszczak, a leader of the Law and Justice Parliament club read a letter signed by the party leader, Jarosław Kaczyński, in which he underlined that to abandon the expansion of OPP would cause economic degradation of the Opole voivodeship, and would result in energy shortages in the country, and the necessity to import it. Kaczyński also mentioned that nearby regions would suffer from energy deficit, and the miners might face lower sale of coal and even closing of the mines. He promised that when the Law and Justice won the election, then one of their first decisions would be the construction of the two blocks. At that moment the politicization of the affair reached the pitch.

On June 10, there was a debate in the tent township in which several energy specialists participated, present were also the MP for Law and Justice, Kłosowski, a former party MP Waldemar Wiązowski, the leader of the Solidarity trade union at OPP, Dariusz Kucharewicz, and others. The debate, moderated by the Opole journalist Bolesław Bezeg, who acted as a secretary of the whole protest action, concluded that the expansion of OPP must be completed because it was an investment important from the viewpoint of energetic security and labor market.

What followed was an extraordinary session of the Economic Commission of the Parliament, on June 20, where the Minister of Finance informed about the expansion. The Prime Minister Tusk and the Minister of Treasury Włodzimierz Karpiński visited OPP on June 27, and Tusk promised that the construction at the value of more than 11 billion PLN would start in summer 2013. It took another seven months before it really happened. In the meantime, the Coal Company (at that time the largest coal mining company in Poland and Europe) signed a memorandum of intention to cooperate with the PGE. The Prime Minister commented that it was a step towards bigger employment and energetic security. Meanwhile, Alstom Power was added to the construction consortium, and the PGE division, PGE GiEK S.A. (Conventional Mining and Energy Sector Joint-Stock Company),[8] informed the consortium about the decision to start the construction. Also the Coal Company signed a contract with the PGE GiEK S.A. about the supply of bituminous coal for the period 2018–2038. During the fall of 2013 two members of the board of PGE, and eventually the CEO of PGE, Kilian, resigned because of differences between PGE and the government. The Prime Minister Tusk commented that energetic companies with financial participation of the state must care for the energetic security of the country. The new CEO of the PGE, Piotr Szymanek, declared on December 6 that the construction of blocks five and six would begin on February 1, 2014. And this really happened on that day. By September 2019 both new blocks were put into exploitation. However, the people of the Dobrzeń Wielki commune participated in the struggle for the expansion of OPP only when they were invited to sign the petition in June 2013 by the organizers of the tent township in Czarnowąsy. Otherwise, it was a struggle fought by the activists from Opole and OPP.[9]

The OPP Enlargement

At the time of OPP's enlargement there was hardly any contact between the leaders of the construction consortium and the leaders and inhabitants of the commune, excepting invitation to celebration organized for a wider audience in summers 2015 and 2016, where the leadership of the commune was present. A couple of project team members also participated in these events. Whereas some of the employees of the OPP were also residents in the commune, the construction consortium hardly employed anybody from the commune. Most employees worked shifts during the

8 In 2012 the OPP lost its separate legal personality and became consolidated with the PGE GiEK S.A.

9 This section is based on the memorandum compiled by Dariusz Kucharewicz and the interview with him that took place in his office on November 2, 2015. See also Czech 2012.

weekdays and went home on the weekends. Thus, also the personal contact between the employees of the construction consortium and inhabitants of the Dobrzeń Wielki commune was minimal. The OPP continued to pay property taxes to the commune during the years of 2015 and 2016. If that continued, the commune would have net profit from the fact that the OPP is located on its territory. In comparison with the original construction of blocks first, two, three and four which lasted for 20 years, the construction of the two more powerful blocks was to take five years only. That made it bearable because the inconveniences connected with the construction would soon be outweighed by tax-paying most modern power station with minimum ecological damage.

Unexpected Turn

Within a month after the elections to the Parliament, which were won by the Law and Justice political party, the research project got an altogether new dimension as a result of the press declaration, in November 2015, of the Mayor of Opole that Opole should expand and de facto annex some villages and adjacent territories including the OPP. The expansion of Opole would also involve some other lucrative establishments such as the shopping mall Turawa (the latter was subsequently dropped from the annexation plan). The Dobrzeń Wielki commune and other communes included into this annexation plan saw it as an attack on their self-government and democracy. They immediately started vigorous protests of its inhabitants and the elected leaders entered negotiations with the Mayor of Opole and other elected organs such as the Parliament of Opole Voivodeship and the Council of Opole District. By the end of April 2016, the voivode appointed by the new ruling party Law and Justice was to give his opinion to the government, which has the authority to change borders between communes. His opinion was in favor of the plan and on July19, 2016 the Polish government took a decision supporting the plan of the Mayor of Opole. The inhabitants of Dobrzeń Wielki received the news with incredulity and therefore continued to protest the decision and for its cancellation. They were supported by part of the press, especially journalists around the Internet portal Balaton Local Group. The Council of the Commune made a request to the constitutional court of Poland – the Constitutional

Tribunal – to block the execution of the decision which was to come into force on January 1, 2017. Also the Ombudsman became involved and gave his support to the cause of Dobrzeń Wielki, however, to no avail.

The land grab was proposed, approved, and carried out. That alienates the lucrative projects such as OPP from the communities which provided territory for their construction. It is the state in conjunction with huge industrial concerns, national or international, which assists in deprivation of local populations of their rights. In that sense, the conducted research project is a case study of the functioning of neoliberal capitalism with its reckless policies of profiteering without respect for the wishes and expectations of people directly involved in the industrial projects. A couple of years after the annexation was carried out, the determination of the inhabitants of Dobrzeń Wielki commune to get justice continues. The question, however, is to what extent those who were incorporated into the city of Opole against their will persist in demanding their civil rights. The communal election that took place in October and November 2018 brought in charge a new leadership. It would be fascinating to monitor how the Dobrzeń Wielki commune would do without the finances from the OPP to which it was used for decades.

The above events raised also methodological problems. Can we keep independence while we see that injustice is being perpetrated and our sympathies lie with people whose rights are being trampled on? Can we be neutral vis-a-vis attempts to limit or destroy communal self-government enshrined in the constitution and laws? Can we look at the abuse of power by political parties when rights and interests of the country or local community are suppressed? These are ethical dilemmas par excellence. But I believe that we should stick to our scientific expertise because it ensures that our authority remains uncompromised and our findings and reasoning unchallenged. The question, however, is to what extent are we able to present our research results to those in power positions. For we cannot be satisfied with our publications in respected journals and books. We want to see application of our findings (cf. Skalník and Brocki 2018).

Conclusion

This chapter has discussed some of the most important political moments which I followed during my field research in the Dobrzeń Wielki commune, and in discussions with other protagonists on the scene of the expansion of OPP. The research clearly showed the key role the power plant has played in the life of the Opole region in the last 46 years. The OPP has proved to have influence not only on its geographical vicinity, but on other parts of the Opole Silesia and even the whole of Poland. The energy security, which in Poland is based on coal, is in apparent contradiction with the EU policy of decarbonization and the global movement in favor of renewable energy resources. Even though OPP is equipped with most up-to-date filters, it continues and will continue to spew out into atmosphere enormous amounts of carbon dioxide. Therefore, continuing to burn coal may cost Poland too much: it threatens to marginalize this country and throw it into a neo-nationalist impasse. The expansion of OPP by two brand new giant blocks is seen locally as a victory for the Opole Silesia. At the same time, it can symbolize the end of the coal epoch in the modern history of Poland. The Dobrzeń Wielki commune has unwittingly played a role far beyond its actual size and importance.

References

Czech, Henryk. "Opolski cud pojednania – rola mitu w sprawowaniu władzy i uprawianiu polityki regionalnej." In: *Antagonizm i pojednanie w środowiskach wielokulturowych*, ed. Jacek Kurczewski, Aleksandra Herman. Gdańsk: Słowo/obraz terytoria, 2012, pp. 145–176.

Czech, Henryk. "Giełczyn (gmina DobrzeńWielki) – dzisiaj." *Societas/Communitas* 1–2 (19–20)/2015, pp. 163–185.

De Rijke, Kim. "Hydraulically Fractured: Unconventional Gas and Anthropology." *Anthropology Today* 29(2)/2013, pp. 13–17.

Dupont, Claire and Sebastian Oberthür eds., *Decarbonization in the European Union: Internal Policies and External Strategies*. New York: Palgrave Macmillan, 2015.

Eriksen, Thomas Hylland. *Overheating: An Anthropology of Accelerated Change*. London: Pluto Press, 2016.

Eriksen, Thomas Hylland. *Boomtown: Runaway Globalisation on the Queensland Coast*. London: Pluto Press, 2018.

Filer, Colin. "Why Green Grabs Don't Work in Papua New Guinea." *The Journal of Peasant Studies* 39(2)/2012, pp. 599–617.

Fortun, Kim. *Advocacy after Bhopal: Environmentalism, Disaster, New Global Orders*. Chicago: University of Chicago Press, 2001.

Fujikawa, Ken. *Environmental Destruction and the Social Impacts of the Fukushima Nuclear Disaster*. Tokyo: Meiji Gakuin University, 2015.

Gill, Tom. "Radiation and Responsibility: What is the Right Thing to do for an Anthropologist in Fukushima?" *Special Issue of Japanese Review of Cultural Anthropology: Practicing a Public Anthropology of the East Japan Disaster* 15/2014, pp. 151–163.

Hasegawa, Koichi. "The Fukushima Nuclear Accident and Japan's Civil Society: Context, Reactions, and Policy Impacts." *International Sociology* 29(4)/2014, pp. 283–301.

Hauhs, Michael and Baltasar Trancón y Widemann, Georg Klute. "Bridging Disciplinary Gaps in Studies of Human-Environment Relations: A Modelling Framework." *Modern Africa: Politics, History and Society* 5(2)/2017, pp. 35–76.

Inose, Kohei. " 'Living with Uncertainty:' Public Anthropology and Radioactive Contamination." *Special Issue of Japanese Review of Cultural Anthropology: Practicing a Public Anthropology of the East Japan Disaster* 15/2014, pp. 141–150.

Ito, Yoko. "EU Policy Background and Realities for 'Coal Phase-out.' " *IEEJ* 12(4)/2017, pp. 1–15.

Kałuża, Ryszard. "Podstawowe wyniki i wnioski z badań i z konferencji naukowej n.t. wpływu Elektrowni 'Opole' na przeobrażenia społeczno-ekonomiczne rejonu i gminy Dobrzeń Wielki." *Zeszyty Naukowe Wyższej Szkoły Inżynierskiej w Opolu* 148(21)/1988, p. 10.

Knudsen, Ståle. "Is Corporate Social Responsibility Oiling the Neoliberal Carbon Economy? Contests over a Power Plant on the Black Sea Coast of Turkey." *Ethnos* 83 (3)/2018, pp. 505–520.

Kokot, Alojzy. "Przemiany społeczno-gospodarcze w gminie Dobrzeń Wielki pod wpływem intensywnej industrializacji." *Zeszyty Naukowe Wyższej Szkoły Inżynierskiej w Opolu* 148(21)/1988, pp. 155–166.

Lesiuk, Wiesław and Robert Rauziński, Teresa Sołdra-Gwiżdż eds. *Między przeszłością i przyszłością: Elektrownia "Opole" jako czynnik zmiany społecznej*. Opole: Instytut Śląski, 2000.

Łuszczewska, Barbara ed. *Elektrownia "Opole" a środowisko społeczne*. Opole: Instytut Śląski, 1993.

Nowakowski, Stefan. *Przeobrażenia społeczne wsi opolskiej*. Poznań: Instytut Zachodni, 1960.

Olszewska, Anna. *Wieś uprzemysłowiona: Studium społeczności lokalnej w powiecie opolskim*. Wrocław: Zakład Narodowy im. Ossolińskich, 1969.

Ossowski, Stanisław. "Zagadnienie więzi regionalnej i więzi narodowej na Śląsku Opolskim." *Przegląd Socjologiczny* 9(1–4)/1947, pp. 73–124.

Parry, Jonathan R. "The Sacrifices of Modernity in a Soviet-built Steel Town in Central India." In: *On the Margins of Religion*, ed. Frances Pine and João de Pina-Cabral. New York: Berghahn Books 2008, pp. 233–262.

Pękala, Józef. "Głos w dyskusji: Przemiany społeczno-gospodarcze w gminie Dobrzeń Wielki pod wpływem intensywnej industrializacji." *Zeszyty Naukowe Wyższej Szkoły Inżynierskiej w Opolu* 148(21)/1988, pp. 5–6.

Projekt polityki energetycznej Polski do 2050 roku. 2015. https://www.cire.pl/pokaz-pdf-%252Fpliki%252F2%252Fpep2050_20150803.pdf. (7 March 2021).

Rosicki, Remigiusz. "The Energy Policy of Poland up to 2050 – A Critical Analysis." *Środkowoeuropejskie Studia Polityczne* 1/2015, pp. 51–62.

Rosik-Dulewska, Czesława and Grzegorz Kusza eds. *Budowa bloków 5 i 6 w PGE Elektrowni Opole SA – aspekty gospodarcze, środowiskowe i społeczne*. Opole: Uniwersytet Opolski, 2009.

Sabela, Tomáš. *Podnikatelé v obci Dobrzeń Wielki*. Unpublished Bachelor Thesis. Pardubice: Univerzita Pardubice, 2008.

Skalník, Petr. "Community Re-studies in Europe and Beyond: Towards a New Concerted Research Initiative." In: *Anthropology of Europe: Teaching and Research*, ed. Petr Skalník. Prague: Set Out, 2005. pp. 117–142.

Skalník, Petr. *Slezská obec Dobrzeń Wielki: Kdo je menšinou (sociálně antropologická restudie)*. Unpublished manuscript, 2007.

Skalník, Petr. "Opakované studie obcí." In *Okno do antropologie*, ed. Petr Skalník and Livia Šavelková. Pardubice: Univerzita Pardubice, 2008, pp. 47–72.

Skalník, Petr ed. *Dolní Roveň: Poločas výzkumu. Dolní Roveň: Research at half-time*. Pardubice: Univerzita Pardubice, 2004.

Skalník, Petr and Marcin Brocki. "Global Anthropologies: Can Anthropologists be Humanizers of Globalization?" In: *Anthropology as Social Critique: Its Public Role in the Globalized World*, ed. Petr Skalník and Marcin Brocki. Cracow: Jagiellonian University Press, 2018, pp. 7–19.

Trigger, David and Julia Keenan, Kim de Rijke, Will Rifkin. "Aboriginal Engagement and Agreement-making with a Rapidly Developing Resource Industry: Coal Seam Gas Development in Australia." *The Extractive Industries and Society* 1/2014, pp. 176–188.

Wallace, Fielding. *Pros and Cons of the Three Gorges Dam*. 2019. https://medium.com/@fieldingwallace/pros-and-cons-of-the-three-gorges-dam-c5e1e9004cea (7 March 2021).

Konrad Górny[1]

Local Community in the Face of Intense Economic Changes: The Dobrzeń Wielki Commune in Opole Silesia

Abstract: This article analyses dynamic transformations launched by industrialization processes in a local community of the Dobrzeń Wielki commune in Opole Silesia with a particular attention given to the Opole Power Plant and its recent expansion. In this context, social and economic changes in the community shaped by the enlargement of the Opole Power Plant and beyond are being discussed both in a historical perspective and in light of the commune's administrative division which threatens its existence as an independent administrative unit.

Keywords: cooperation, industrial investment, local community, local economics, social conflict.

Introduction

One of the constitutive features of ethnology is speaking about reality through the description and analysis of specific cases, and not building broad theories of various social phenomena. This approach was also used in this text and is mainly related to the empirical nature of the field research to which the content of the article refers. Such a position is characteristic of all ethnology, in which scientific theories are built rather cumulatively over long periods of time. Thus, it can be said that knowledge in this case usually grows without breakages reversing up its entire order, and that it does not happen that important discoveries or interesting ideas disappear along with the criticism that affects the theoretical

1 Department of Ethnology and Cultural Anthropology, University of Wroclaw, konrad.gorny@uwr.edu.pl, ORCID: 0000-0002-6965-1608.

and methodological orientations "generating them" (cf. Brocki, Górny 2010: 186).

Among the countless issues that are related to the above thesis, there are also studies of local communities recognized as a research category and a certain comprehensive social structure, consisting of many components such as a common territory, relatively limited number of members, close social contacts, permanent social ties, common local organization, or at least partial dependence on larger territorial communities. The above-mentioned elements appear in most definitions of such social microstructures, and their most characteristic features emphasized by most researchers are supposed to be local ties and local forms of organization of collective life, which play an important role in binding and intensifying various activities undertaken by the members of a given community. They are also significant when it comes to accelerated modernization processes and changes connected with them, whose success depends on, among others, social assessment, and acceptance in the local environment. The ability to act together is extremely important in this case and almost always depends on social cohesion closely related to internal systems of dependence and institutions (see e.g. Bednarski 1987: 150–153).

The contemporary local community does not resemble a traditional community and it is based mainly on the local government community model, of which typical is an openness to the outside world, manifesting itself, for instance, in not impeding the inflow of new and outflow of former members of a given local system. This is accompanied by active participation in various areas of communal life and preservation of strong identification with one's place of residence. Thus understood, local communities are structures open to changes to which they have been subject to various degrees and on many different levels for several decades (Starosta 2006).

The above type of local community became a focus of intensive fieldwork research conducted by a research team of the University of Wroclaw and the Jagiellonian University in Cracow in the Dobrzeń Wielki commune in the central part of Opole Silesia in south-western Poland. The frame was provided by the research project entitled *Conflict, Tension, Cooperation: A Study of Interaction between the Opole Power Plant and the Community of the Dobrzeń Wielki Commune.*[2] This research explored and analyzed multidimensional and interrelated cultural, social, political, and economic processes taking place in the commune, mostly in relation to the ongoing expansion of the Opole Power Plant (OPP) located within its administrative borders. In this chapter I discuss economic changes that have been taking place in the Dobrzeń Wielki commune since the turn of the nineteenth and the twentieth century but intensified significantly with the start of the above-mentioned expansion. In particular, I am interested in how the dynamics of these changes have affected the local community of Dobrzeń Wielki. To this end, I analyze the subsequent stages of industrialization in the commune and its influence on local economy with a special attention given to the OPP as an important agent shaping local forms of social and economic life. The proposed analysis has been based on the fieldwork research conducted together with Mirosław Marczyk as a part of the above-mentioned research project. It focused on economic issues and involved dozens of conversations and unstructured interviews with the inhabitants of the commune regarding changes in the local economy in relation to the operation and expansion of the OPP.

The Dobrzeń Wielki Commune in a Historical Perspective

The researchers of the analyzed region emphasize that both the village of Dobrzeń Wielki and other villages forming the commune has been undergoing intense social transformations since the late nineteenth century. Their causes lie mainly in the processes taking place in the wider world, and they were primarily nascent capitalism and the industrialization associated with it (Nowakowski 1960: 8). It is believed that the first "opening" of the community to the outside world and the beginning of broadly understood modernization processes was undoubtedly influenced by the construction of a highway and a railway line which connected Dobrzeń Wielki with the neighboring big cities: Opole and Wroclaw. It also had an impact, along with

2 The project was implemented from August 2014 to January 2019 at the University of Wroclaw with Petr Skalník as the Principal Investigator. It was financed by the National Science Center, grant number 2013/11/b/HS3/03895.

shipping on the Odra River, on the development of economic migrations, not only to the above-mentioned cities but also to Western Europe (Nowakowski 1960: 23). These trips are being undertaken by the residents of the commune to this day. An important moment for the inception of the process of transformations related to industrialization was the construction of a river shipyard in 1906 (the village of Dobrzeń Wielki is located on the bank of the Odra River), dealing mainly with the production of transport boats. The shipyard has operated successfully for over 100 years but has recently declined and its potential has not been appreciated and sufficiently used, which forced the last owner to significantly reduce its activities. In addition, in the interwar period, craftsmanship and small trade began to develop in the Dobrzeń Wielki commune, with the most numerous being carpentry and wicker workshops, producing furniture (Nowakowski 1960: 24). As a curiosity we can treat the information that before Second World War there were 10 inns in the village of Dobrzeń Wielki, which is an impressive number compared to the one restaurant that currently operates there.

The socio-economic changes found an expression in the spatial layout of Dobrzeń Wielki, which is the largest village in the commune and at the same time the seat of the communal authorities. What is interesting, already in the 1950s Stefan Nowakowski, a sociologist and researcher of the villages of Opole Silesia, wrote that Dobrzeń Wielki had twenty-nine streets and resembled a small town rather than a village (Nowakowski 1960: 32). He also stressed that urban influences were very much visible in Dobrzeń Wielki, especially in the economic life, which, for those times, was saturated with modern technology (Nowakowski 1960: 35). It can therefore be concluded that the process of changes related to urbanization or at least partial industrialization in the area of the described commune was something permanent and lasting at least from the end of the nineteenth century. However, it should not be forgotten here that, despite the above-mentioned changes related to the economy, the sphere of family and neighborhood life was described as quite traditional, closely related to the strong role of the family and the church as institutions exerting the greatest influence on social and cultural life (cf. Nowakowski 1960: 37).

The open character of the discussed community was undoubtedly influenced by economic migrations, the beginning of which dates to the nineteenth century, when many, especially young people, started cyclical trips to work in Germany.[3] As already noted, this type of back-and-forth labor migrations are a characteristic feature of economic strategies undertaken by the residents of the commune up to the present day. The economic transformations mentioned above had consequences in social life. It can be stated that already at the turn of the nineteenth and twentieth centuries a group of rural industrialists was formed in the commune, who, being owners of craft workshops or shops, lived equally well or better than the owners of large farms. Moreover, in the interwar period, individual owners of a shipyard, brickyard, small textile factory, sawmill, owners of large transport boats, restaurants and shops etc. began to create a new social class that was gaining more and more importance in the social structure of the commune. Changes of this type were also accompanied by progressive ties, especially economic, of villages with wider supra-local structures (until 1945, mainly within the German state).

Another period of socio-cultural and economic changes began with the end of Second World War and the accession of Silesia to the Polish state. It is a particular time, as there was a change in the existing social order, and the post-war chaos was accompanied by intense migration processes and the transformations in the structure of the local population occurring simultaneously and on many levels. One of the consequences of the then change of state borders and the change of the political system was the cessation of systematic economic emigration to Germany and job search throughout Silesia, and the commune itself began to function as a local labor market. From the construction of the first post-war knitting factory, employing nearly a thousand workers, mainly women, the industrialization process of the countryside began, bringing along further changes in the lifestyle, generating new, economic, and cultural needs of the residents (cf. Nowakowski 1960: 213, 215). The more and more intensive process of the introduction of elements of urban culture became a characteristic phenomenon in the lives of rural residents. It was a global phenomenon, which took on specific forms in the Dobrzeń Wielki commune in the

3 Broadly understood nationality issues are not the subject of this chapter, but we should also consider their impact on some transformation processes, especially those related to labor migrations and their local specificity. These issues were first described in detail by Stanisław Ossowski (1947).

following years, especially when the OPP, one of the largest power plants in Poland, was built here.

Already in 1969, justifying the choice of the research area, a well-known Polish sociologist wrote about Dobrzeń Wielki that although it was an agricultural commune, it represented an urbanized community, especially in the economic, spatial and social spheres, which brought the village closer to urban-industrial structures (Olszewska 1969: 7). The same author, on the basis of her own research in the Dobrzeń Wielki village, was the first one to put forward a hypothesis that an urbanized village can successfully compete with the nearby city as a living and residential environment. What is interesting, she also noted that the living conditions in Dobrzeń Wielki were better here in material and landscape terms than in the nearby city if Opole (Olszewska 1969: 66). In this way, the currently visible urban character of Dobrzeń Wielki is nothing new and should not be associated only with the wealth of the inhabitants related to the circular economic migrations to Germany or the Netherlands. The same applies to the construction and expansion of a coal-fired power plant, which only strengthened the industrial and urban character of the village and a large part of the commune. The construction and operation of the knitting factory, which belonged to the largest factories of this type in Poland in the 1950s and 1960s (more on this issue see Olszewska 1969: 71–108), should therefore be considered the first and significant element of industrialization, causing a series of socio-cultural changes in the commune in the postwar period. The location of Dobrzeń Wielki in the vicinity of the city also made it a village in which a relatively large percentage of residents were employed in industry. As a well-known researcher of this region believes, it was a typical feature of many areas of broadly understood Silesia, where old and new structures coexisted quite often (Olszewska 1969: 141–142). Such a situation had to lead to a progressive professional and socio-economic diversification of the population, strengthened by constantly ongoing labor migrations.

Subsequent transformations in the Dobrzeń Wielki commune landscape, as well as in the socio-cultural and economic structure, began with the construction of the OPP named after the nearby city of Opole. Its construction took twenty years, from 1973 to 1993, so the investment began in the real socialism, and was completed in the first years of the so-called political transformation, that is, the period of transition from a centrally controlled economy to an economy dependent on the laws of the so-called free market. The entire process was thus very time-consuming and happening at the time of both economic and political changes, which caused it to leave a strong mark on the local community in which it was taking place. It was also significant that the decision to build such a large industrial investment had been made without any public consultations. The spatial local system, in which the landscape of the commune was completely dominated by the infrastructure of the power plant and related companies, had been transformed. A new housing estate "Energetyk" was also built in the village of Dobrzeń Wielki for the incoming employees of the power plant, which clearly stood out from the previous buildings, and the fact of isolating this space was further intensified by the location of the estate away from the central part of the village. The long-term process of building the power plant was very negatively assessed by the residents of the commune, but the commissioning of the OPP in the mid-1990s, in the period of increasing unemployment in Poland, gave hope for the development of the commune and improvement of the existence of its inhabitants. Since that time, the OPP became one of the largest industrial plants in the Opole voivodeship in terms of concentration of workplaces (Kałuża 1993: 129). Nowadays, the power plant continues to play the role of a potential employer, and the increased role of the local labor market has become one of the factors of integration of various population groups, both local and from other regions of Poland (cf. Kałuża 2000: 64).

Therefore, the OPP can be considered one of the most important factors in the broadly understood social change that took place in the local community of the discussed commune. However, the construction of the power plant was not the last element influencing the rapidly changing socio-economic situation of the commune and its residents. The next part of the transformations began with the decision by the Polish government to significantly expand the OPP, which became one of the largest industrial investments in Europe. Thus, such a large investment could not remain without impact on the local community and not cause a wave of further changes in the local economy or social structure.

OPP Expansion in the Eyes of the Local Community

Since 2013, that is, from the moment when the final decision about the power plant's expansion was made, the OPP has once again become the most important reference point for economic strategies undertaken within the local community, generating a new wave of changes that could potentially be a source of tension, conflict, or cooperation. Those phenomena were the main subject of the aforementioned fieldwork research, and part of that research was conducted by the author of this article and concerned potential changes in the local economic system.[4] Since modernization processes had been occurring in the discussed area for many years, the research interests encompassed phenomena related not only to the expansion, but also to the construction and operation of the power plant. However, the most important remained mutual relations between the plant's expansion and the local community, who had high expectations connected with that particular investment. From the very beginning it was hoped it would become the main factor of the commune's development. As a major investment and a gigantic material object, the OPP has become the dominant "co-inhabitant" of the local world. It has radically modified the cultural landscape, also through the network of companies, enterprises and industrial plants that grew up in its close vicinity, and the flourishing of various economic activities, directly or indirectly related with the operation of the power plant, as well as with its expansion.

In the generally outlined network of local economy, the research area was heterogeneous, despite the dominant role played by the OPP. The activities of economic entities established mainly due to cooperation with the power plant were of a different nature than those which benefited from this cooperation to a lesser extent or not at all. Striking and contradictory to the research intuition was the fact that there was little development of local entrepreneurship, aimed mainly at the benefits of the expansion itself, which turned out to follow patterns other than those known from the time of the construction of the power plant. The main difference in this case was that most of the elements needed to build new power units were

4 Information not referenced in bibliographic sources comes from materials collected during the above-mentioned ethnographic fieldwork research.

produced outside the commune, sometimes in other countries, from which they were transported and assembled on site. In such a situation, one could get the impression that two different and completely separated social and economic realities existed side by side. One included the power plant and the adjacent areas, the other the remaining areas of the commune, with people dealing with their own affairs, living at their own pace, independent of the expansion.

In this case, the visible isolation of the construction site from rural life was decisively influenced by processes taking place in the global sphere, including the possibility of the flow of technology and its products in a short time and over long distances. As a result, this led to the exclusion of local communities from the implementation of industrial investments for the benefit of environments where the production costs of individual structural elements were lower, or the search for specialized contractors in distant countries. Low price and professional specialization played a key role in this case, treating local environments as less important for the implementation of the investment. This also applied to costs related to employment, and more specifically to "cheap labor," as a typical phenomenon for the Polish labor market at that time, where specialized agencies were ready to bring employees from distant parts of the country and from abroad, should the costs of employing local employees turn out to be high. This happened, for example, in the case of the extension of the OPP, where a large group were workers from Ukraine. It should be added that the expansion began at a time when the phenomenon of the lack of workforce, which has been noticed in the domestic market in recent years and is associated with a dynamic decline in unemployment, did not yet occur.

The changes that accompanied the above-mentioned phenomena took place at the intersection of political and economic relations, revealing over time their links with the development of the OPP, taking the form of new economic strategies undertaken by the residents of the commune. It was a process that influenced the lives of the residents in a multi-level way, both individually and as a group. The image of the community at that time was created in a specific socio-cultural landscape, characterized by a mixture of rural, suburban, and industrial elements. It was possible to obtain it by listening to what local residents had to say about it. In their statements, they portrayed the commune and its transformations in a favorable light, and showed the specificity of the place where they lived and worked. Research has revealed, for example, that the changes taking place can also be described by analyzing the processes of gentrification and its effects. This process continued in the commune uninterrupted, and intensified during the construction of the OPP, resulting in an influx of new, usually better educated people, affecting the local economy and its segments. The consequences of this were changes in the social structure, in the spatial arrangement of the commune, changes in the lifestyle of the residents, the emergence of specific relations between the groups of the incumbent local population and the gentry. This was well illustrated by the above-mentioned construction of the "Energetyk" housing estate intended for power plant employees, who were initially viewed with distrust. However, over time the antagonisms subsided and, as a result of various activities and integration processes, a sense of community was formed stemming not only from the place of residence, but also from sharing similar values (cf. Berlińska 2000: 89–98).

The functioning and expansion of a large industrial investment resulted in the emergence of phenomena that could cause tensions and potential conflicts. Such was also the nature of the decision to extend the power plant itself, not preceded by wider public consultations. This failure to take into account the opinion of the residents was often emphasized in the talks, although at the same time there was an awareness of the need for expansion, which had been planned for a long time. As expansion became a reality, there were many concerns about the various possible consequences associated with this kind of investment. The point of reference for this type of opinions was the experience of residents during the construction and commissioning of the power plant. It was usually remembered as a time of chaos and pathological behavior on the construction site and its surroundings, as well as a period of intense influx of aliens and devastation of the natural environment. It should be emphasized that the related memory was mythologized and passed down through the generation that witnessed those events. Stories of this type are still circulating in society and have contributed to an exaggeration of the image of similar threats expected in the expansion of the power plant.

The uncertainty of many residents of the commune was intensified by the closely watched political discourse on the issue of expansion. The changing positions of successive authorities at the state level regarding the decision to continue with the expansion or to abandon it questioned the purposefulness of local economic initiatives aimed at potential profits from participation in the broadly understood process of expansion of the power plant. Another issue was, for example, concerns related to the nationwide discussion on the construction of a nuclear power plant and the abandonment of the development of coal-based energy. Some interviewees feared that the decision to expand was short-sighted, believing that Poland would eventually be forced to build a nuclear power plant. There were also opinions suggesting that this was a purely political and economically unjustified decision.

On the other hand, the use of coal technology caused concerns about environmental pollution and its impact on life and health, and some of the concerns known from the time when the investment was created returned. People who commented on this topic often did not trust the assurances about the high security of the technologies used. For example, it was emphasized that the groundwater level dropped significantly, which was associated with the decline of agriculture in the commune. It was believed that the power plant was "poisoning" the residents and polluting the area. Some people observed that morbidity had increased in the area. There was also talk about the adverse effects of the magnetic field around transmission lines, and the potential to cause asthma, cancer, and allergies, especially in children. Residents also noticed the phenomenon of a specific microclimate, which was to be characterized by a reduced amount of rainfall. At the same time, there were also contradictory statements, pointing to the improvement of air quality resulting from access to the heating network, and thus – liquidation of small boiler houses which would burn low-quality coal fuel or simply rubbish. It should be added that many such opinions were based on the residents' negligible knowledge about the technologies used at the plant.

The expansion also brought about other types of concerns about the environment: increased car and rail traffic, high air pollution, and degradation of roads caused by heavy road transport were mentioned in the first place. The village of Brzezie, located in the closest vicinity to the OPP, was the most exposed to any inconvenience associated with the expansion. It was also the only location from which some of the residents were evicted.

This procedure was motivated by the immediate vicinity of newly built cooling towers, which were to limit access to sunlight, and even deprive some households of it. An increase in noise and dust levels was also forecast. The residents of the village, despite their reluctance to move out and disputes over the valuation of their property, received long-negotiated financial compensation for their losses and for the abandoned buildings.

An extremely important problem highlighted by most of the interviewees was the anxiety about the expected influx of workers from various parts of the country and from abroad. Those fears were twofold. Firstly, people feared the arrival of strangers who were unfamiliar with the local sociocultural specificity and therefore potentially a source of threat. Secondly, an increase in crime or even ethnic conflicts were predicted. Fears of this type resulted mainly from the experience of the construction of the OPP, which resulted in the influx of people from various parts of Poland. These newcomers penetrated the structures of this area and began to change them, despite their ignorance of the so-called a Silesian lifestyle, characterized by calmness, order and high respect for work, according to the local population. From conversations with the residents, it can be concluded that the acculturation process has never ended and continues to this day, and the expansion of the OPP may entail a repetition of the phenomenon of the influx of foreigners. The first symptoms were noticed very quickly, and they concerned foreigners, mainly Ukrainians. It should be noted, however, that these fears turned out to be unjustified. The incoming workers were also perceived as competition on the local labor market, which was supposed to provide employment mainly for the local population. The related tensions could, however, be limited by the phenomenon of rural depopulation, which ran parallel to the influx of people interested in working and living in the commune. Mostly young people left the commune, benefiting from family contacts in Germany or the Netherlands, thus causing the aging of the commune's population, which was noted by one of the local parish priests as a noticeable decrease in fertility, visible from his perspective in the decreasing number of baptisms and communions.

A characteristic feature of the local labor market during the research was the belief that foreigners would occupy the most attractive jobs in the OPP, perceived as one of the most reliable employers in the region. Furthermore, work at the power plant was widely assessed as very attractive. In addition to the conviction about relatively high earnings that can be achieved there, great importance was attached to the stability and security of employment in the place of residence, providing various types of financial benefits and the prospect of a high pension. Hence, such opinions were often accompanied by the belief that it was extremely difficult to find a job at the power plant and that it could only be guaranteed by personal or family connections, but once you got a job, people's lives changed significantly. Very good earnings, training, holiday subsidies are just some of the features praised by people who talked about working in a power plant. The expansion of the power plant itself aroused similar emotions, but the research also revealed the ambivalence of attitudes, which was visible among many residents of the commune. Some were looking for benefits that they could gain directly or indirectly, others were critical and did not see any profits for themselves and the commune resulting from the investment.

The quotation of negative or positive aspects of the OPP operation and its expansion was accompanied by neutral opinions, often associated with the lack of recognition of the relationship between the wealth of the commune and the power plant, which in this case was perceived as one of the elements of the landscape that had to be accepted. Mutual dependencies between the investment and the local community were rationalized and based mainly on common knowledge and common reasoning. Their feature was primarily the expectations and ideas expressed by the inhabitants. During the research, opinions were also noticed that the expansion of the power plant would not change much, and the commune authorities should focus more on the protection and fate of permanent residents. Hence the view that the management of the power plant influenced the local authorities by not fulfilling the promises to which it should have been obliged when taking over the OPP. This includes, for example, the development of a heating network, reduction of electricity prices, and even the development of a training system for local youth that would allow them to work and take up positions in a power plant. It should be noted that these were ideas resulting from the perception of the OPP as a guardian who, due to its location in the commune, was obliged to support the local community. For many years, the OPP had been fulfilling this task through various activities, and primarily through financial support. However, this cooperation was interrupted with the change in the location of the power plant management, which was moved to the city of Bełchatów, where the headquarters of the Polish Energy Group (PGE) is located. Whereas the OPP became a part of the PGE already in 2007, in 2012 it was consolidated with the PGE division, PGE GiEK S.A. (Conventional Mining and Energy Sector Joint-Stock Company), and lost its separated legal personality. This change has significantly influenced the relationship between the OPP and the local community. The cooperation known from the past, when the power plant was an independent unit, directly supporting local initiatives, was not longer possible. Its scope became strongly limited and influenced the perception of the OPP, which was now treated primarily as a payer of high taxes, some of which could be used to finance the needs of the commune's residents.

Division of the Dobrzeń Wielki Commune

On the basis of the residents' statements, it can be concluded that the OPP turned from being a "co-inhabitant" of the local world to something like a separate entity isolated from the social space. This industrial structure is visible from almost every place in the commune, completely dominating the local landscape. In a long process of changes, it was in a sense "domesticated" and accepted, but by bringing extremely high financial profits for the commune it also became the subject of interest of the authorities of the nearby city of Opole, and one political decision destroyed the former state of affairs. This decision was related to the so-called Plan of Great Opole whose aim was to increase the administrative territory of the city by incorporating 12 neighboring villages (including those of the Dobrzeń Wielki commune) to enhance its economic growth. The residents of Dobrzeń Wielki commune first learned about the plan of commune's division from an article published in the *Nowa Trybuna Opolska* (New Opole Tribune) daily in November 2015 (Zyzik 2015). The article was an interview with the Mayor of Opole, who presented the plan of expanding the city, justifying it with the necessity to develop Opole. This plan quite accurately defined the new city limits, the course of which in the Dobrzeń Wielki commune was delimited in such a way that the OPP and most of the large industrial plants cooperating with it and located in its immediate vicinity would now fall within the city limits of Opole.

Hence, from the very beginning this plan was perceived as “robbing” the commune of the richest investment areas and called a “money heist.” To the surprise of the residents, about 90 percent of whom expressed a negative opinion about this project, a few months later the application for the enlargement of the city of Opole with selected areas of neighboring communes was transferred to the government level. For the residents of the Dobrzeń Wielki commune, it was a decision that meant the loss of several villages, including the most important one from an economic point of view, Brzezie, where the OPP and most large enterprises operated. The long-term plans for the economic development of the commune were therefore questioned, and the protest against the planned division became a part of the residents’ lives for many months, continuing with varying intensity until today. To this day many residents believe that the strategy of Opole’s authorities aimed at appropriating the commune’s space and had the hallmarks of an institutional intervention that radically changed the existing redistribution of goods, thus impoverishing the residents. The motives for these activities were not perceived as a necessity of the territorial development of the city or the good of larger social groups, but as a simple acquisition of material resources and income of the commune.

The desire to break up an efficiently functioning local community, an integral part of which is the native Silesian population and the German minority, sensed by the residents and the commune’s authorities, was also important. This community had already incurred large material, social and environmental costs related to the construction of a large investment in its area, and when it started to develop dynamically, using the funds from this investment, the community was deprived of them. It is therefore not surprising that the commune authorities, with a full, almost 100 percent support of the local community, took several actions aimed at defending the territorial status of the commune and respecting the civil rights of its residents. This situation resulted in a spontaneous, grassroots social reaction of opposition, which took many different forms: demonstrations, pickets, road and office blockades, or hunger protests, during which the terms “occupiers” or “annexation” were often used in relation to the city authorities. Flags, banners, and posters informing about the views of the residents and their opposition to the decisions made behind their backs have almost permanently appeared in the landscape of the commune. In this way, the local community entered the next stage of changes, this time political, but strongly influenced economically. The operation and expansion of the power plant then began to be played between the authorities of the Opole voivodeship and the city of Opole, the government, and the community in which it was located. This uneven game ended with the incorporation of these parts of the commune into the city of Opole. Since the beginning of 2017, the Dobrzeń Wielki commune has been operating within the new, reduced borders, its funds have impoverished and to a large extent have become dependent on the financial aid of the city of Opole, which was guaranteed only until 2020. In such a situation, questions arise about the future of the commune, its survival as a separate administrative unit, the quality of life, and the possibility of undertaking business activities in new conditions. The future will show whether the new economic problems of the commune within its new borders will be somehow resolved. The key to the success of remedial actions may be an effective restructuring of the commune, considering the economic and social aspect in equal measure.

Even at the end of 2016, when the major field explorations of the economic module were ending, the residents of the commune considered their success the harmonious coexistence and cooperation of the indigenous and immigrant population, manifested in cultural and educational activity, projects for the quality of life in a shared space, and even political activity. However, the compact social tissue was broken, and there were contradictory opinions about the attitude to the purposefulness of the changes taking place, which was manifested, for example, in discussions on the improvement/deterioration of the quality of life within the new administrative borders of Opole and the territorially limited commune of Dobrzeń Wielki. Thus, the expansion of the OPP, previously perceived as a development investment, eventually became the cause of the problems of the commune, which – until recently one of the richest in Poland – currently hovers on the edge of survival as an independent administrative unit.

Conclusions

One of the well-known Polish sociologists, for whom the Dobrzeń Wielki commune was the subject of scientific interest, wrote that Dobrzeń Wielki was "a unique village because it is difficult to find another such place in Poland that would be of constant interest to subsequent generations of researchers from 1945" (Berlińska 2000: 89). Most of these researchers noticed that the residents of the commune had been subject to numerous processes of transformation for a long time, at least from the end of the nineteenth century, among which changes in the economic sphere played an extremely important role (cf. Nowakowski 1960: 230–238). As a result of those transformations, in the mid-twentieth century Dobrzeń Wielki reached the level of an industrialized village, and already then, the local community was perceived as progressive, as people were using the most modern appliances in their households. Moreover, it was a wealthy village that owned its wealth not only to large farms, but also to profits from employment in industry. This related to the circular economic migrations to Western Europe or other regions of Poland, influencing the dynamics of socio-cultural changes, which, interestingly, did not take place rapidly here and did not significantly modify the strict family and neighborly ties or attachment to broadly understood local traditions. Thus, the image of the commune, inhabited primarily by a specific Silesian community, rooted for many generations, emerges from numerous sociological works (cf. Berlińska 2000: 92–93).

When we look at the location of the OPP and its subsequent expansion in the socio-cultural environment defined in this way, the decision to take back this investment and everything related to it appears to be an extremely dramatic event. For the first time in the recent history of the Dobrzeń Wielki commune there have been and are still ongoing economic changes, the direction of which is unknown or significantly regressive. It was the result of political decisions that were taken over the heads of the local community, a fact of which most of its members are now aware. It is evident in the research of the project team (e.g. Skalník 2018), but also in the recently published research by sociologists from Opole. The latter one pertained to opinions of the residents of the suburban communes, 80 percent of whom assessed the expansion of Opole negatively (cf. Myczka 2019). The OPP is no longer the "key player" and the driving force of the economy, however, as a major industrial investment it permanently transformed local systems and threatened the stable existence of the local community. A question remains as to how this community will manage in new conditions, whether its previous "resourcefulness" allow the Dobrzeń Wielki commune to survive this crisis, and whether the trust to the institution of state can be rebuilt. The residents, accustomed to the fact that their commune has been in a very good economic condition for many years, will have to face the problem of underinvestment, lack of innovation or inability to construct far-reaching development plans, known from other regions, which may be an extremely interesting topic for further in-depth research on this a community, which is a favorite of various researchers.

References

Bednarski, Jacek. "Grupa lokalna." In: *Słownik etnologiczny: Terminy ogólne*, ed. Zofia Staszczak. Warszawa: Państwowe Wydawnictwa Naukowe, 1987, pp. 150–153.

Berlińska, Danuta. "Integracja społeczna mieszkańców osiedla 'Energetyk' z zasiedziałą ludnością Dobrzenia Wielkiego." In: *Między przeszłością a przyszłością: Elektrownia "Opole" jako czynnik zmiany społecznej*, ed. Wiesław Lesiuk, Robert Rauziński and Teresa Sołdra-Gwiżdż. Opole: Instytut Śląski, 2000, pp. 89–98.

Górny, Konrad and Marcin Brocki. "W stronę konkretu – powrót czy kolejny zwrot w etnologii?" In: *"Zwroty" badawcze w humanistyce: Konteksty poznawcze, kulturowe i społeczno-instytucjonalne*, ed. Jacek Kowalewski and Wojciech Piasek. Olsztyn: Instytut Filozofii Uniwersytetu Warmińsko-Mazurskiego w Olsztynie, 2010, pp. 185–192.

Kałuża, Ryszard. "Sytuacja na rynku pracy w rejonie oddziaływania Elektrowni 'Opole'." In: *Elektrownia "Opole" a środowisko społeczne*, ed. Barbara Łuszczewska. Opole: Instytut Śląski, 1993, pp. 123–136.

Kałuża, Ryszard. "Rola Elektrowni 'Opole' na rynku pracy." In: *Między przeszłością a przyszłością: Elektrownia "Opole" jako czynnik zmiany społecznej*, ed. Wiesław Lesiuk, Robert Rauziński and Teresa Sołdra-Gwiżdż. Opole: Instytut Śląski, 2000, pp. 59–65.

Myczka, Leszek. *Odtajnione wyniki badań Danuty Berlińskiej: Wiśniewski i Czubak powinni się wstydzić*. 2019. https://opowiecie.info/odtajnione-wyniki-badan-danuty-berlinskiej-wisniewski-czubak-sie-wstydzic/ (28 Nov. 2020).

Nowakowski, Stefan. *Przeobrażenia społeczne wsi opolskiej*. Poznań: Instytut Zachodni, 1960.

Olszewska, Anna. *Wieś uprzemysłowiona: Studium społeczności lokalnej w powiecie opolskim*. Wrocław: Zakład Narodowy im. Ossolińskich, 1969.

Ossowski, Stanisław. "Zagadnienie więzi regionalnej i więzi narodowej na Śląsku Opolskim." *Przegląd Socjologiczny* 9(1–4)/1947, pp. 73–124.

Skalník, Petr ed. *Mutual Impact: Conflict, Tension and Cooperation in Opole Silesia*. Wrocław: Uniwersytet Wrocławski, 2018.

Starosta, Paweł. "O pożytkach płynących z badania społeczności lokalnych na podstawie programu Polska Lokalna." In: *Społeczności lokalne: Teraźniejszość i przyszłość*, ed. Bohdan Jałowiecki, Wojciech Łukowski. Warszawa: Scholar, 2006, pp. 83–106.

Zyzik, Krzysztof. *Prezydent Wiśniewski chce powiększyć Opole*. 2015. https://nto.pl/prezydent-wisniewski-chce-powiekszyc-opole/ar/9103027 (28 Nov. 2020).

Mirosław Marczyk[1]

Bottom-Up Economic Strategies in the Light of the Opole Power Plant Expansion

Abstract: The article concerns relationships between the expansion of the Opole Power Plant and economic bottom-up activities undertaken by residents of the Dobrzeń Wielki commune, which were shaped by various cultural, social, and political forces. In this context, the author discusses differentiated strategies of small and large entrepreneurs shown as immersed not only in the specific local contexts, but also as in many ways related to supra-local processes and phenomena.

Keywords: economic strategies, entrepreneurship, industrial investment, local community, local economics.

Introduction

Bottom-up social and cultural activities are often perceived as initiatives undertaken outside of formalized institutions, serving to construct a social world and an individual or local identity. It is also agreed that these activities are associated with various political, social, or economic phenomena occurring both on a regional and national scale (more on this issue see Cichocki et al. 2015). It is in reaction to those types of phenomena that activities which can be called bottom-up are undertaken. They take form of various cultural activities, among which bottom-up economic strategies are of key importance. Impulses for those activities are provided by specifically targeted social changes. In Poland, they began after 1989 along with political and economic transformations. The result of these changes was engagement in various bottom-up adaptive activities, which became the subject of anthropological research and its results have already been

1 Department of Ethnology and Cultural Anthropology, University of Wrocław, miroslaw.marczyk@uwr.edu.pl, ORCID: 0001-6441-9327.

published (see e.g. Buchowski 1997, 2018; Kuligowski, Stanisz 2017; Rakowski 2009).

Along with the progressive course of changes and the influence of broader processes of a globalizing nature, there were changes in economic activity, in which the share of persons who most often started one-man or family businesses was visible. Similar phenomena were occurring in the Dobrzeń Wielki commune in Opole Silesia in southern Poland, which at the turn of the 1980s and 1990s experienced problems connected with the closing of workplaces and growing unemployment (Kałuża 2000: 59). Small trading and service companies, especially those established after 1989, were developing slowly and only some of them managed to remain on the market or expand their operations. The situation changed when construction of the Opole Power Plant (OPP) commenced in the commune in the mid-1970s, and the plant, put to work in the mid-1990s, became a source of rapid modernization processes. Thanks to them the commune was systematically losing its previous agricultural character, becoming an area dominated by industry and trade and service economy. Already in 2000, several large businesses were operating in the commune, which was recorded in sociological research (see e.g. Lesiuk 2000: 8).

The emergence of the OPP caused several changes in the environmental landscape and initiated a process of establishing new forms of entrepreneurship, from companies strictly connected with the power plant to various businesses meeting the needs of new residents of the commune, who came from different parts of the country to work in the OPP. Over time, the network of connections with the power plant at its center began to be visible. From its assets, due to the privatization processes, so-called daughter companies were separated and eventually became independent. At the same time, larger industrial plants were set up to use the by-products generated as a result of the coal combustion process and other plants not related to the operation of the OPP. These companies are the main source of employment for the residents of the Dobrzeń Wielki commune and the surrounding area. The potential associated with the operation of many business entities became one of the foundations for the development of small entrepreneurship. The number of small retail and service companies is much higher in the commune than in the neighboring communes and it determines its economic potential. This network has been forming for many years, and in many cases the entrepreneurs saw a chance for its further development in the expansion of the OPP planned for the years 2014–2019.

In this chapter, I analyze the dynamics of the bottom-up economic strategies of the above-mentioned networks of local entrepreneurs in the Dobrzeń Wielki commune, which emerged due to the expansion of the OPP. The empirical material was gathered as a part of the team research project entitled *Conflict, Tension and Cooperation: A Case Study of Mutual Impact between the Opole Power Station and the Community of Dobrzeń Wielki.*[2] The intensive ethnographic field research on the economic issues in the commune was conducted together with Konrad Górny between 2014 and 2016, that is, at the peak period of work related to the expansion of the OPP. The field material was obtained in the course of talks with residents of the commune, especially those involved in various economic activities. These conversations, often in the form of non-standardized and unstructured interviews, concerned business activities, their types, local specificities and conditions, and especially the relationship between running a "business" and the functioning and development of the power plant. Furthermore, the public documents, available in the archives and partially on the website of the Commune Office were analyzed. These comprised, alongside others, statistics on local entrepreneurship and the structure of financial income and expenditures of the Dobrzeń Wielki commune. The field material gathered in the first stage of research was later verified in 2017 and 2018 to check how the progress of the OPP's expansion and an unexpected change of administrative borders of the commune in 2017 shaped bottom-up economic strategies.

---

2 It was implemented at the University of Wroclaw from August 2014 to January 2019 with Petr Skalník as the Principal Investigator and financed by the National Science Center (grant number 2013/11/b/HS3/03895).

Local Forms of Economic Adjustment

The expansion of the OPP, which involved the construction of its fifth and sixth blocks, and at that time was one of the largest investments in the energy sector in Europe, raised expectations connected with the economic development of the Dobrzeń Wielki commune and of the businesses operating within it. However, reality proved to be different, as the expansion of the OPP turned out to have no decisive influence on the functioning of the local economy. The connection of the major industrial investment with the local community proved only indirect, and local business operators were forced to seek common areas of investment which would allow them to use the expansion to their own advantage. Many local entrepreneurs managed in the new situation and recognized that potential financial gains from the expansion of the OPP could be obtained primarily from the two aspects of economic activity: services and trade.

The service business primarily involved renting apartments and lodgings to other companies, which booked accommodation for their employees depending on how time-consuming the work was. Their stays took many weeks, months or even longer, which guaranteed stable and predictable profits. Sometimes these companies did not pay attention to the standard of services offered, although the managers expected higher quality of accommodation and access to high-speed Internet, for example. The rental price was a matter of direct bargaining and the profits were assessed as high. Service providers faced competition, which sometimes led to misunderstandings. As a result, there was a phenomenon of accommodation providers accusing each other of hiding the actual number of persons staying overnight and, consequently, the actual revenue.

The residents of the community have adopted very different strategies when it comes to renting accommodation. Very few hotel accommodations have been built or renovated. The existing buildings and residential space were used predominantly. Only small repairs and alterations were made on an ongoing basis and the rooms were equipped at the lowest possible cost. There were even owners of grocery stores or bars, whose business had declined due to the expansion of chain stores. Therefore, in search of new sources of profitable income, these people were converting them into accommodation. The residents were aware that the demand for rental offers was temporary and would fade as the development progressed and eventually end after the new blocks were put into operation. For this reason, excessive investment in the construction of new facilities, renovation and modernization of housing was neither profitable nor necessary, as each offer was met with enormous interest from companies that preferred to pay larger amounts of money rather than face the costly transportation of workers to the power plant from distant locations. The renovation of the workers' quarters and the construction of hotels were associated with an increased demand for construction work. For this reason, companies trading in building materials, interior furnishings, window carpentry, electrical installations, offering television services, servicing roller blinds, windows, electric gates and the like had significantly more orders. In turn, owners of local companies interested in renting apartments or hotel rooms, e.g. for their guests and contractors, noticed that the housing market in the Dobrzeń Wielki commune, but also in Opole, "strongly shrank" and prices rose significantly. Thus, their companies' operating costs have increased.

Observing the strategies adopted within the development of the accommodation base, a clear division was noticeable into two segments of activity, one being temporary, and the other one based on a long-term, thought-out business plan. An example of this could be the operation of two hotels, each of which had adopted a different model of functioning and development. The owner of the Pod Kominem Hotel, located in close proximity of the OPP, used the economic situation of the moment and spent a significant part of income from the room rental on modernizing and raising the standards of provided services. At the outset, these services were targeted mainly at people working at the construction site of the new blocks of the power plant and characterized by a low standard of dormitory-type rooms. However, modernization allowed to improve the quality of services to such an extent so that once the development of the power plant was completed, the target customers of the hotel included management staff, guests or various types of experts working for the OPP.

The situation was different in a hotel located in Dobrzeń Mały, another village forming the commune. It was built from scratch just before the expansion of the OPP began, and its owner decided to use subsidies from the EU. In this case, taking advantage of the current economic situation consisted in obtaining funds which would allow to pay off the loans and continue the operation of the hotel after the expansion. It should be emphasized that the quality of the services offered was already high, and the owner was planning on expanding it by a recreational section. Here the target group were supposed to be tourists, especially members of families who had emigrated to Germany and who were now eager to visit their homeland. Another important part of the activity was the organization of various kinds of special events.

Trade was considered yet another aspect of profitable activity. Increased revenues were expected especially in the food industry. It was hoped that the workers employed at the construction site would shop in the stores operating within the Dobrzeń Wielki commune. It did happen, but trade was almost monopolized by chain stores and markets such as Dino, Biedronka, or Tesco, and so small, family-owned stores were only slightly affected by the economic upturn. However, exceptions from this rule could be found which point to the ability to adapt to changing conditions. For instance, the owner of a butcher shop in the village of Borki said that she sold much more to individual clients, and she also took delivery orders from some companies. Among her customers there were also foreigners hired at the expansion of the OPP. From her perspective, what was important was the quality of offered goods, because regional and natural products, especially those that did not contain preservatives, were very popular among clients. The owner of one of the family-owned grocery stores adopted a different solution in the face of increased competition. She changed her line of work and started selling shoes, which turned out to be an extremely successful undertaking. It should be added that the store also sold online, which shows innovation and coping skills in changing business environment. Therefore, also in this case more or less accurate strategies based on economically justified decisions counted the most. A very important aspect which affected the reduction of costs of running a business was its location on one's own property, which is very common in the case of Dobrzeń Wielki commune. Usually, the location was the decisive factor in starting the activity: the closer it was to the main communication routes, the better.

Gas stations were exceptionally satisfied with the expansion of the OPP. Recognizing that they were dealing with constructors of new blocks of the power plant was not a problem, as they required invoices. They recorded a significant increase in demand, and hence turnover and profits. They needed to adjust quickly to the new situation by changing the assortment of goods offered in their own convenience stores. This concerned seemingly unimportant details, such as introducing large size of coffee packs instead of small, because the new customers expected that. Small local transportation companies, which mainly worked for the OPP, were also using the gas station.

The influx of workers expanding the power plant also resulted in increased demand for catering services, but observations during the study indicated that owners of local restaurants or small catering outlets did not significantly increase their revenues. It should be remembered that workers mainly used canteens located near the OPP and prepared meals on their own, which resulted from savings and access to kitchens at places of accommodation. It is also important to note that large restaurants did not adapt their offer to the new conditions, which could have consisted of offering cheap meals to employees of companies or the construction consortium that were the main contractors of the expansion project. For this reason, the residents of the Dobrzeń Wielki commune were still the most frequent customers, and, according to the owners, the custom of family dining in restaurants at weekends or on holidays has been systematically disappearing. The main profit was made from wedding receptions and other family and special events.

Other beneficiaries of the expansion of the OPP included companies dealing with advertising services, production of banners, signs, and the like. For them, the power plant has always been a good customer, and the arrival of new businesses at the expansion provided another opportunity to increase profits. Although some companies brought promotional materials with them, many entrepreneurs outsourced their production to local, even quite small, businesses.

Another example would be garages, although in this case the situation was ambiguous. Increased revenues were recorded especially by the garages located in a visible, well-marked place. One of the owners stated, for example, that the number of individual clients from different parts of Poland and abroad has increased. He managed to establish cooperation with several companies working for the OPP and provided them with car repairs and other services. New customers were often forced to use his services due to the long distance from their place of residence or company registration. He was one of the few respondents who recognized their reliability. He explained that this was due to the nature of the consortium implementing the expansion of the power plant, which monitored contractors, and if they happened not to meet certain requirements, contracts with them could be terminated. Such subcontractors were therefore not random, and the selection made by the consortium was considered a guarantee that local companies would also be paid fairly and on time. In a similar way, the Regional Vehicle Inspection Station in Czarnowąsy, which handled a large proportion of the trucks used in the expansion and those registered in companies cooperating with the OPP, significantly increased its profits. The situation was similar in other, but not all, car and repair workshops, especially those located on the sidelines. Examples of disappointed hopes for increased income could be seen in statements indicating that not many new customers appeared. They showed up sporadically and expected cheap, quick, temporary repairs only in case of emergency breakdowns. Thorough repairs and modernizations were done in their places of residence, especially when they moved around by their company cars.

The prosperity favored local firms engaged in training, consulting, health and safety inspection and supervision, design, and construction supervision, working with subcontractors and the OPP expansion contractors. In this case, the good economic climate brought an increased number of orders and financial revenue. Since many more people began to pass through the commune, even the photographic studio, whose customers were incoming workers from Poland and abroad who ordered photographs necessary for issuing various documents, recorded profits. The increase in sales also concerned household appliances. A haberdashery store and a garden design company also gained new clients.

Large and Small Businesses

People who did not live in the Dobrzeń Wielki commune, but only run their business activity there, expressed positive opinions about its development, high living standards and infrastructure. The commune compared favorably with the neighboring communes or even the city of Opole. The wealth of the commune was mainly associated with the OPP being located on its premises and considered as a guarantor of financial stability. In this way, the commune became an attractive partner for entrepreneurs using a variety of amenities and the orders it placed. In other parts of the Opole region such a situation was rare, which should not come as a surprise since the Dobrzeń Wielki commune was the richest rural commune in the region. However, this situation was not without its problems.

Due to its direct participation in the expansion and earlier construction of the OPP and its role in the local community, the Kociok company deserves special attention. Its owner developed his own business while the power plant was still under construction. He was prompted to do so by his personal observations of the construction site, where he worked for a short time. According to him, what was noticeable at the time was, above all, a lack of work organization. This observation and his experiences during a visit to Germany, where he encountered completely different standards, led him to set up his own company, which soon received its first orders from the power plant during its final stage of construction. As soon as the company learned of the expansion, it began preparing to participate in tenders issued by the construction consortium managing the investment. They consisted in purchasing new equipment or increasing employment in order to meet the high competition on the market. An unquestionable advantage of the company was its location in close vicinity of the construction site, which made it possible to significantly reduce labor costs and offer cheaper services. As a result, the company won a number of tenders related to, for instance, earthworks and was treated by the construction consortium as the one to be used in emergencies, for the so-called intervention works.

It may be added that the owner, foreseeing the complicated process of acceptance of the performed orders, the necessity to issue payment certificates, took care to provide financial reserves allowing for smooth operations. The owner's reflections on the attitudes of the commune's inhabitants, who almost did not benefit from the fact of locating the OPP in their vicinity, seem also interesting. They did not try to derive any profits from it, even ignoring employment offered by companies involved in the expansion process. The proposed salaries were considered too low and the work too hard, counting on lucrative jobs in Germany, for example, so the company was forced to hire specialists from outside the commune.

This problem was also raised by owners of other companies, noting the phenomenon of lack of manpower, as the manager of a company engaged in the sale and installation of windows:

> To be honest, there's a problem with professionals, we're actually waiting for them to arrive. Because in this region there are major problems with finding people for work. I know it can be a matter of money and so on, but even when it comes to young people for jobs that do not require any bigger knowledge or skill, there's still a problem with finding workers. So they bring people from abroad, mostly from Ukraine, that's better for us that we have more hands for work.[3]

Kociok was an example of a dynamically growing company, skillfully taking advantage of the opportunity to earn income from work carried out on the expansion of the OPP. This was one of the reasons why the company has grown steadily, even though according to the owner only around 30 percent of the company's capacity was generated by work on the expansion, especially towards the end of the investment period. This shows that most of the business activity was conducted not only in the OPP extension and in the commune, but mainly on the supra-local market. This is therefore a very good example of how a bottom-up economic initiative was transformed, through cooperation with a power plant, into a company for which the local market became too small and did not ensure that the company's potential is fulfilled.

This problem also applies to several other large companies for which the Dobrzeń Wielki commune was no longer an economic partner. Their owners, with dozens or several dozens of employees, held it against the commune that while they contributed large amounts of taxes to its budget, they were still not taken seriously and were subject to numerous restrictions. In their view, they were wrongly accused of overexploiting and damaging roads, generating nuisance noise, smoke, dust and degrading the commune's environment. Some entrepreneurs stated that they were even suggested to limit their activity, and they pointed out that the commune authorities were supposed to be favorable only to those residents who valued a peaceful, rural model of life above all or treated the commune as a "bedroom" community. Hence, this group of entrepreneurs more often expressed the opinion that the commune administration was slowly

3 All unreferenced quotations originate from the field materials.

ceasing to be an attractive business partner for them, preferring instead persons running small business, e.g. service business, for which the commune in turn created excellent conditions.

Let an example of the above situation be the statement of a person comparing the treatment of her by officials in Opole and Dobrzeń Wielki. Not only did this person not receive proper assistance from city officials, but she was also informed about various problems accompanying the establishment of her own business in the industry she proposed: "Why do you want to run something like that? Do you know how harmful it is for the city? Do you know these services can be a disturbance? Do you know you'll need consents from the neighbors? Do you know you'll need permits from the environmental protection section?" In the same situation, the officials from the Dobrzeń Wielki commune acted quite differently:

> I came to the Commune Office and I said I was going to look for a piece of land and ... open such and such line of business. Would you like me to get the head of the commune? Please, do come in. I went in and I tell him what this is about. Madam, we will do everything to make this easier for you. I will appoint a person who will guide you through this. We are very happy that such a business will run in the area because we do not have one yet. We will help you a lot. He went with me to the construction department, he appointed a person to help me, and that person really did guide me by the hand through everything. After three months, I have everything. Construction permit included. Do you see the difference? Because I do ... you have an issue, you go to the right window in the office, you tell them what your problem is, please sit down, I will help you, this is what I'm here for. They have the time, they have the will.

A good example of discrepancy between large and small entrepreneurs was the assessment of the construction of the planned ring road around five communal villages located along the national road No. 454 and how its functioning would affect business activities conducted in these villages. In this case, fears were voiced by owners of small businesses located primarily in the immediate vicinity of the road. They were convinced that the decrease in road traffic would cause a substantial decrease in the number of customers, a reduction of income from sales or services, and may pose a threat to their operations: "Once they build a ring road, Dobrzeń Wielki will be a regular, poorly developed village, off the beaten track, the expansion of the power plant will only bring losses, or nothing will change. We have fewer and fewer customers; our store is the last one in the village." In a different way the creation of a ring road was assessed by large entrepreneurs, especially those whose activity was dependent on the ease and speed of transport and communication. In this case the ring road would promote mobility and reduce costs, so from this perspective it was an expected and desirable investment.

It is worth adding, that when talking about issues related to communication and transport, the residents of the Dobrzeń Wielki commune noticed missed opportunities related to the possibility of using the Odra River. It is a natural waterway running through the territory of the Dobrzeń Wielki, which remains underappreciated. Inhabitants did not understand why coal delivered to the OPP was transported by rail and all deliveries by road. Decision makers were accused of failing to take steps to restore water transport, to modernize the port that operated here in the past. Some residents recalled the times when barges on the Odra River transported coal from Upper Silesia and back upstream, they carried river silt, which was later used to fill the passages in the mines. The recently repaired sluice located near the village of Chróścice, where several community residents found work, was seen as a harbinger of change in this regard. It could be assumed, as local entrepreneurs claimed, that the opening of the river port would increase the economic potential of the commune.

Specificity of the Dobrzeń Wielki Commune

The extension of the OPP definitely influenced the development of entrepreneurship in the Dobrzeń Wielki commune. A large industrial investment became a reason for and an opportunity to restructure the existing economic potential, which was particularly well illustrated by the dynamics of the establishment and reorganization of actual businesses. Their number was estimated at almost one thousand, with a vast majority of private companies, most of which were small, often one-person businesses. However, the statement that such bottom-up economic practices undertaken in the local community were related only to the expansion of the OPP is not justified. Also, the only seemingly visible consequence of the new investment was the creation and development of an accommodation base for construction workers, employees of the consortium and the OPP, or increased demand for services and trade. Considering the mutual relations between the local community of Dobrzeń Wielki commune and the OPP, it can be concluded that its long-term functioning in the commune was much more important than the expansion itself affecting the local environment over the past few years. It was primarily the construction and functioning of the power plant, and not its extension, that has left its mark on the history of the commune and its contemporary times. A sudden increase in the number of inhabitants, and thus an increase in demand for services and trade, has released the potential and creativity of local, bottom-up economic initiatives. This concerns particularly the models of functioning of economic initiatives, thoughtful and economically justified undertakings supported by courage in decision making, resourcefulness and conviction about their effectiveness.

The cultural environment in which the described processes took place was not without significance. For this environment, identity, and adherence to certain values, such as attachment to the inhabited space, community, or work ethos, were significant. Therefore, the effective implementation of economic strategies was influenced by the "entrepreneurial habitus" associated in this case with the incumbent population of Silesian origin or the German minority community. Such an observation undoubtedly requires in-depth comparative studies.[4] Meanwhile it should be noted that this group brought into the Dobrzeń Wielki commune certain models which were not commonly known in the Polish cultural landscape after 1989. This concerned in particular the models of economic initiatives, well thought-out and economically justified undertakings supported by courage in decision-making, resourcefulness, and conviction of their effectiveness. The residents acquired these skills while working, for example, in Germany and other highly developed Western European countries, where they had contact with a different system of work organization, the relationship between its quality and remuneration. Equipped with this knowledge, they could easily meet the requirements imposed on them by the systemic change in Poland. An important role in this case was also played by the fact that they had accumulated capital abroad, much of which could be invested in their own businesses in the place of residence. Even in the event

4 Similar issues were noticed during the studies on the impact of the A2 motorway on local cultural landscapes (Kuligowski, Stanisz 2017: 316).

of the failure of such ventures, they had the option of returning to their previous way of life, that is, going abroad to earn money. Moreover, when they returned home, they brought with them the experiences and standards of living observed abroad, which contributed, for example, to the modernization and expansion of their own surroundings and environment.

Similar Western European patterns and high standards were applied to the models of governance and management of the Dobrzeń Wielki commune, which modernized at a rapid pace. This would not have been possible, however, if it were not for the very good financial condition of the community, which was greatly influenced by the presence of the OPP on its territory. The consistent economic policy of the local authorities, skillful disbursement of financial resources and long-term action plans were conducive to the location of new companies in the commune and, consequently, to the creation of new jobs and many bottom-up initiatives. All such phenomena created an inseparable network of economic ties and consolidated the ways of capital flow between large industry, the local financial resources, and small entrepreneurs. The related economic successes of the commune translated directly into a high quality of everyday life of its citizens and attracted an increasing number of new residents interested not only in living in a well-kept and socially friendly commune, but also in locating their own businesses there.

Thus, the economic relations between local entrepreneurship and the functioning and expansion of the OPP, which were decisive for the community's existence, determined the specificity of socio-economic ties and bottom-up economic activities undertaken within them. This specificity also influenced the development plans prepared in accordance with long-term strategies by the local authorities. It should be added that such long-term planning was possible due to the predictable and stable financial revenues, among which the key importance was attached to tax revenues paid by the power plant and large enterprises located in its vicinity.

Economic Aspects of the Commune's Partition

The above-mentioned stable network of connections between various types of institutions in the commune was interrupted when a sudden and unforeseen decision was made at the supra-local level to incorporate a large part of the commune into the city of Opole. Motivated by the need to obtain new investment areas, the Mayor of Opole's decision was accepted by the government, and its consequence was the loss of five villages by the Dobrzeń Wielki commune. Their size constituted about 30 percent of the commune's area inhabited by a comparable percentage of the population. The territory incorporated into the city included the OPP and many industrial plants that had previously constituted the economic potential of the commune. From the point of view of the local economy this was an unprecedented event, as it disturbed and even destroyed the social and economic order that had been developed over many years. There was also a threat of the emergence of phenomena which might affect the lives of the residents of the commune in a multilevel and sudden way. This indeed happened. The budget deficit of the diminished commune meant that without external one-time subsidies in 2017 and 2018, the commune would face bankruptcy. According to the predictions of local authorities, without radical financial cuts and limiting or abandoning planned investments, the existence of the commune as an independent local government unit came into question. Layoffs of employees in the Communal Cultural Center and the Commune Office started already in 2017, teachers were deprived of relatively high motivational bonuses, the support subsidies for care and educational centers and scholarships for pupils were significantly reduced or canceled, the number of sports instructors was reduced, and the plan was abandoned to subsidize the replacement of obsolete furnaces with modern heating systems. What is more, the commune was deprived of attractive investment areas. The spatial development plans have also lost their validity.

The decisions made at high levels of government and imposed from the top down without any public consultation, thus forced and unexpected, led to a dramatic situation. As a result, the prosperous and richest rural commune in the Opole region was degraded to a commune with a peripheral character, facing problems it had not experienced for many years. The consequence of this state of affairs was the necessity to develop new strategies aimed at the survival of the commune in the new conditions. If the new strategies proved impossible to implement for various reasons, the commune was threatened with bankruptcy. The decision at the beginning of 2016 to divide the commune and annex its considerable area to the city of Opole was interpreted very negatively by the majority of residents and treated as an unjustified interference in their lives and achievements as a local community. This resulted in lengthy protests in defense of the unity of the commune and its citizens, a social space that should remain intact as one of its fundamental values. For this reason, a struggle was launched to stop the process of dividing the commune, even at the cost of giving up the huge financial revenues from the OPP. So far, the actions of local and regional leaders have not been considered significant; the policy of the central authorities, not taking into account the dynamically changing economic reality of the commune, turned out to be more important.

However, according to the research conducted in 2017, the change of the commune boundaries did not significantly affect the scope of activities of local entrepreneurs, who indicated only minor inconveniences related to the need to change documents, information on advertising folders and websites. However, they emphasized the possibility of the emergence of threats resulting from the functioning of the so-called business environment when its base for many of them became not a rich commune, open to initiatives, but a poor one or a large city with a complicated administrative and organizational structure. Important in this case was also the upcoming completion of the OPP development process and, consequently, the shrinkage of business ventures related to this process. The first symptoms of this situation were already visible in 2017 and in 2018 in the form of limited demand for goods and services. A good example to illustrate this phenomenon were requests from small entrepreneurs to the management of the above-mentioned Pod Kominem Hotel, which due to the OPP's vicinity still had customers, to re-locate some of the guests to local lodgings as their owners were unable to repay the loans taken from banks and intended for the construction and operation of the accommodation. The possible bankruptcy of many local small businesses, along with a dramatically reduced communal budget, was a premise for the probability of economic regression of the Dobrzeń Wielki commune and shows how short the road from rapid economic development to stagnation can be.

Conclusions

Research conducted in the Dobrzeń Wielki commune has shown that a large industrial investment promotes the formation of a complex network of connections between local and supra-local economies. The analyzed dynamics of the bottom-up strategies of local entrepreneurs in the Dobrzeń Wielki commune, which emerged due to the expansion of the OPP, brought tensions and conflicts not in those contexts where they could be initially expected. On the one hand, the relations between the OPP and the construction consortium carrying out the extension works, the communal authorities and local entrepreneurs were conducive to the establishment of various forms of cooperation. They definitely resulted in modernization impulses favorable for the commune's development. However, the local community, and particularly some entrepreneurs, did not feel to participate in this general well-being to the degree they had previously expected. The specific model of management, which underlaid the OPP extension, made it a phenomenon separated from the everyday life of the Dobrzeń Wielki community. However, the most serious conflict situation arose unexpectedly not because of the interference of big industry, but of the state authorities whose intrusion in the administrative structure of the commune made its economic future uncertain. These developments may constitute an extremely interesting subject of the further research.

References

Buchowski, Michał. *Reluctant Capitalists: Class and Culture on a Local Community in Western Poland*. Berlin: Centre Marc Bloch, 1997.

Buchowski, Michał. *Czyściec: Antropologia neoliberalnego postsocjalizmu*, Poznań: Wydawnictwo Naukowe UAM, 2018.

Cichocki, Piotr and Karolina J. Dudek, Tomasz Rakowski, Sławomir Sikora, Katarzyna Waszczyńska, Anna Wieczorkiewicz, Magdalena Zatorska. *Oddolne tworzenie kultury: Perspektywa antropologiczna*, Warszawa: Instytut Etnologii i Antropologii Kulturowej UW, 2015.

Kałuża, Ryszard. "Rola Elektrowni 'Opole' na rynku pracy." In: *Między przeszłością a przyszłością: Elektrownia "Opole" jako czynnik zmiany społecznej*, ed. Wiesław Lesiuk, Robert Rauziński and Teresa Sołdra-Gwiżdż. Opole: Instytut Śląski, 2000, pp. 59–65.

Kuligowski, Waldemar and Agata Stanisz. *Ruchome modernizacje: Między Autostradą Wolności a "starą dwójką."* Warszawa: Książka i Prasa, 2017.

Lesiuk, Wiesław. "Przeszłość i współczesność okolic Dobrzenia Wielkiego w badaniach Państwowego Instytutu Naukowego – Instytutu Śląskiego w Opolu." In: *Między przeszłością a przyszłością: Elektrownia "Opole" jako czynnik zmiany społecznej*, ed. Wiesław Lesiuk, Robert Rauziński and Teresa Sołdra-Gwiżdż. Opole: Instytut Śląski, 2000, pp. 7–12.

Rakowski, Tomasz. *Łowcy, zbieracze, praktycy niemocy: Etnografia człowieka zdegradowanego*, Gdańsk: Słowo/obraz terytoria, 2009.

Marcin Brocki[1]

Revival of Local Identity Under Political Pressure: German Minority in Southwestern Poland

Abstract: This article discusses ethnic divisions in the Dobrzeń Wielki commune as a part of political dispute over changing commune's administrative borders which triggered a social crisis. A small and ethnically diversified local community was struggling to build unity when it had to face a politically inspired attack from the national government with purpose of deciding on local issues from a position of strength. While the government tried to fit its narrative into the ethnically framed "us" vs. "them" division, at the time of the crisis this provoked a sense of unity across the existing divide and endowed local community with new signs of identity rooted in common agency.

Keywords: German minority, ethnicity, local community, politics, social conflict.

Research Site

This article will address the results of ethnographic research on the revival of ethnic divisions discourse in southwestern Poland, near the city of Opole, in the Dobrzeń Wielki commune. It is important to notice that the area belonged to Germany until 1945. Today about 60 percent of the local population are indigenous residents of Silesia (Silesians, German-Silesians), and within this number about 20 percent admit its German descent (Lis 2016: 186), although they were unable to manifest their separate identity until the beginning of 1990s and post-socialist Poland. Only one of the villages in the commune was settled in by Poles from the former

1 Institute of Ethnology and Cultural Anthropology, Jagiellonian University in Cracow, marcin.brocki@uj.edu.pl, ORCID: 0000-0003-3703-9761.

Polish eastern borderland territories (Ukraine nowadays), who admit their cultural differences with the indigenous population.

The commune is industrial and agricultural in character, with the Opole Power Plant (OPP) being its largest industrial facility. Although unemployment in the commune is marginal, many people leave for Germany or the Netherlands for better paid work, both seasonally and living a two-home life. This is especially true for persons who hold both Polish and German citizenship. Migration of various kinds is relatively easy and massive in this area, as in the whole area that belonged to Germany before the Second World War, because the autochthonous people and their descendants are covered by special legal regulations.[2]

I have conducted my ethnographic research in the area since 2004, with some breaks. So far, I have investigated the ethnic relationships in the Dobrzeń Wielki community, "continuity and change," the way in which the local community experiences the effects of social, economic, and political transformation in Poland since 1989, and the effect of the

2 The most important post-war documents regulating Polish-German relations with regard to citizenship are: 1) the Basic Law of the Federal Republic of Germany of May 23, 1949, which granted citizenship to so-called refugees and expellees of German nationality, their spouses and children who found admission on the territory of the German Reich as of December 31, 1937; 2) Resolution of the Council of State No. 37/56 of May 16, 1956; 3) "The Treaty of Warsaw" between West Germany and the People's Republic of Poland, signed by Polish side on December 7, 1970, by Germany on May 17, 1972; 4) Judgment of the Federal Constitutional Court on the treaties between the Federal Republic of Germany and the Union of Soviet Socialist Republics and the People's Republic of Poland on the foundations of the normalisation of their mutual relations of July 7, 1975, in which it is stated that the Federal Republic of Germany is legally obliged to treat persons of German nationality coming from the eastern territories as still possessing it; in other words, persons arriving in Germany as "displaced persons" or "late displaced persons" were treated as native Germans; 5) Convention between the People's Republic of Poland and the German Democratic Republic on the regulation of cases of dual nationality of November 12, 1975 (Kijonka 2013). The above regulations were the legal foundation for various forms of migration of the Silesian and German populations between Poland and Germany, particularly intensive since the 1970s.

expansion of the OPP[3] on the local intergroup relations. The latter one is the main subject at present since 2015. I assumed that the expansion might influence mutual intergroup relations in the Dobrzeń Wielki commune, because those remained tense at least since the end of the Second World War. Social problems related to the construction and extension of the OPP have already been studied (Kokot 1988; Szmeja 1988; Woźniacki 1988; Biela 1993; Czech 2009; Malarski 1995; Rauziński 1995), but the ethnic context of those problems was somehow overlooked.

The present article is based on research that I undertook within the framework of team research project entitled *Conflict, Tension and Cooperation: A Case Study of Mutual Impact between the Opole Power Plant and the Community of Dobrzeń Wielki.*[4] In my part of the project, I focused on the above-mentioned interethnic relations and the current expansion of the power plant. However, very soon after I had started my research, "ethnicity" became the center of a political dispute, although the fuel of the dispute came from outside and unexpectedly with the project to enlarge the city of Opole at the expense of Dobrzeń Wielki commune. Because the social and political situation in the commune was very dynamic, I had to adapt my research tools and introduce more informal, ad hoc strategies based mainly on semi-structured interviews accompanied by many informal talks and participant observations of both everyday activities and special events of different kinds, such as formal gatherings of the Commune Council, events organized by the OPP management, and informal meetings of friends. However, supplementary data was collected on the basis of the vast sociological literature related to interethnic relations in the area (e.g. Ossowski 1947; Nowakowski 1960; Frysztacki 1998; Szmeja 1997) and development of the local community (e.g. Olszewska 1969; Berlińska 1998).

3 The construction of the fifth and the sixth blocks of the OPP took place between 2014 and 2019. At that time, it was one of the largest investments in energy sector in Europe.

4 The project was implemented from August 2014 to January 2019 at the University of Wroclaw with Petr Skalník as the Principal Investigator, and financed by the National Science Center, grant number 2013/11/b/HS3/03895.

Throughout 2016 to 2019 one could observe a social crisis in the community caused by political factors, namely the government's decision to enlarge the city of Opole and include neighboring villages from, among others, the commune of Dobrzeń Wielki into the city's administrative boundaries. My research strategy had to change, and the research had to be extended to the developing crisis situation. The existing theories of interethnic relations and the knowledge about their course in the studied region had to be expanded with theories of social crises, one of which was just unfolding before our eyes. There are number of conflict and crisis theories in anthropology, of which the most famous is certainly the one originating from the so-called Manchester School. In the discussed case, the one proposed by Victor Turner seemed to fit the situation in commune the best. Turner (1975: 35–42) shows that the crisis is a moment when meanings culminate, and norms are exposed. During the "social drama" the parties can define a situation, to name and frame it, that is, to turn a hard-to-understand tension into concrete. This is exactly the course of the crisis in the commune of Dobrzeń Wielki I have observed. It has created nearly laboratory conditions for the analysis of many diverse phenomena, among which are local identities and intergroup relations.

What Is this Conflict About? An Introduction

In November 2015 the authorities of the city of Opole announced in the local newspaper (*Nowa Trybuna Opolska*) their intention to annex part of the commune, including the most profitable industry in the region, the OPP, into the city of Opole. The appropriate forms were submitted to the Voivodeship Office, which is supervised by the state administration, and to the relevant ministry without prior consultation with local authorities or communities. Polish legislature permits such a procedure, that is, voivodeship and state authorities are allowed to change the administrative borders of self-governmental units and while social consultations are required, they are often purely advisory in nature. On January 1, 2017 Polish government issued the legal regulation on establishing the borders of certain communes and towns, granting some localities the status of a town and changing the name of some communes. Among the changes approved already in 2016, those concerning the Opole Voivodeship (more precisely the city of Opole and the Opole district) were indicated (Choroś, Skrabacz 2017: 162).

Two factors made the situation in the Dobrzeń Wielki commune special compared to other similar changes introduced with the help of the above government regulation. Firstly, the disconnection of a highly profitable industrial complex for the commune, and secondly, interference in fragile ethnic relations, as the Opole region is the main place of residence of the German minority in Poland.[5] Worse still, it is the latter factor that has begun to be used by the government side to achieve its political goals. Majority of inhabitants of the local community of Dobrzeń Wielki commune protested against the state taking away part of their commune and against the procedure behind this process. I believe that it is precisely this last element, namely, the fact that the voice of the people who were affected directly by the changes of commune borders was disregarded, that is the key to understanding any social processes in the commune, because it is not the only case when the local voice was silenced by the ruling majority depriving local people of agency.

Because the different forms of protest, from blocking the roads, through gatherings in Opole in front of the Mayor' premise, to attempts at reaching the relevant Minister, were fruitless, the community decided to begin a hunger strike, which also proved ineffective. The case was submitted to the Constitutional Tribunal, a Polish constitutional court that, unfortunately, has recently become a politicized façade, and to the European Parliament as well as to the European Court of Human Rights – all for nothing. The EU institutions were also not only the last instance in the chain of local counteractions, but the first instance that German minority leaders turn to as a model institution that secures proper standards of democracy and minority rights from the beginning of their public presence. This was exemplified by a slogan used in political campaigns: "We are the bridge to EU" (Lis 2013: 187). Thus, how is the current conflict related to intergroup

5 It may be worth adding that all communes, parts of which were to be incorporated into Opole, were communes with a German minority, the splitting up of which threatened to deprive them of their previous rights to the German language as an auxiliary language in government offices and to bilingual signs with village names.

relations, how does it affect local identity? At this point, I must sketch an overview of the origin and stages of the conflict.

The Conflict's Origin and Stages

If one will accept an "emic" perspective on ethnicity, for instance, in the version proposed by Stanley Tambiah (1996: 138–139) that emphasizes bottom-up substantialization and reification of qualities and attributes by mythohistorical charters and claims of blood descend related to specific territory that establishes historically and politically flexible ethnic boundary, then the complicated ethnic situation in the region will become clearer. Before Second World War the commune was dominated by an indigenous Silesian population that spoke Polish dialect (Nowakowski 1960: 39), although during the Upper Silesia plebiscite in 1921 the majority (about 70 percent) decided to remain within Germany. Under Nazi administration, the majority in the commune declared their German descent, but on the contrary, just after the Second World War the majority declared their Polish descent. There is nothing unusual about this – it is a typical example of the strategic identity of border communities (see e.g. Lis 2016). Already Stanisław Ossowski, an outstanding Polish sociologist and author of the first post-war sociological study on the inhabitants of Dobrzeń Wielki, noted that in this area the foundation of identity was localness, and the broader ethnic identity and nationality were more a strategic choice than a strongly internalized and integrated set of attitudes and perceptions (Ossowski 1947), which is also confirmed by authors of later studies (Nycz 2010; Simonides 2004). Thus, declarations of national or ethnic affiliation were forced on the local population on the occasion of censuses and could not be of any other than strategic nature.

Unfortunately, the same was true of the local authorities, which were not elected from among the indigenous population either but were imposed from outside. This state of affairs lasted until the early 1990s (Lis 2013: 167). Local relations were shaped by many factors, from big politics, through everyday acts of overt or covert differentiation to banal nationalism,[6] which, according to the indigenous inhabitants of the commune, resulted in discrimination against local Silesians in the public space and

6 A term introduced by Michael Billig (1995) in his book with the same title denotes a range of ordinary, everyday practices, symbols, emblems, objects of

relegation of localness to the private sphere and a closed circle of friends. The local languages, both the Silesian dialect and the German language (often referred to as "community own languages"), were eliminated from public space. Interestingly, before the Second World War, Silesian dialect was banned for similar reasons, as a variety of Polish. These factors support Silesian distrust and a sense of harm and deprivation of agency which is present in the local community for generations.

Repeated sociological studies of the Dobrzeń Wielki commune have shown that intergroup relations have been shaped by such correlates of consciousness as language, regional origin, historical fate, and individual experiences, which define the framework of group memory. It is worth mentioning here that young people from the non-indigenous population when asked about broader than personal identity, mostly expressed their national identity and did not identify with or feel an emotional connection to the region, unlike the local Silesian population. Against the background of the above-mentioned correlates of consciousness, Germans were close neighbors of Silesians, they were familiar, while Poles seemed foreign, they were not understood, they were called Ukrainians (Sołdra-Gwiżdż 2010: 138–139, 228). It should be acknowledged that political emancipation or even visibility of Germans, Silesian-Germans in the public sphere was not only prohibited by the state regulations but the majority's commonsense knowledge and social memory also limited its presence. As Joanna Jasiewicz (2015: 1585) notes, In Poland

> The memories of the Second World War intertwine particularly strongly with the German minority's present, limiting the scope of the ethnic leaders' public action. As surveys from the 1990s clearly show, fears that the Germans would reclaim Polish western territories were widespread. I argue that the symbolic link tying the German minority to the perpetrators of atrocities during the war creates taboos that maintain symbolic boundaries of speech and identity. These taboos prevent the German leaders from openly addressing the recognition of past injustices suffered by the group after the Second World War.

---

everyday use, such as identity cards, local currencies or even the structure of news programmes, which remind us of national identity and perpetuate a sense of national community.

Despite quite recent regaining a certain sense of agency, the feeling of being dominated by an alien group has still not disappeared. According to some authors, this feeling is so strong that it overshadows other dimensions of social life, resulting in a specific ethnic orientation and national option, that is, opting for German identity (e.g. Szmeja 2000: 192). As Danuta Berlińska (1998: 34), a sociologist working in the area for many years, explained

> Losing war resulted in the Germans experiencing an identity crisis and the Silesians searching for new identifications. In a confrontation with Poles, Silesians found that although before the war they had not been German enough to be considered German, after the war, their cultural otherness expressed in, e.g., their dialect "contaminated" with German disqualified them as Poles and made them vulnerable to constant discriminatory practices as an "insecure element." As a result of Polonization pressure (speaking German was after the Second World War prohibited) and discriminatory practices, the isolation between the Silesians and the Poles deepened, and the former's subjective feeling of proximity to Germans was increasing. Those processes contributed to subsequent waves of emigration to West Germany. Those who stayed used isolationism as a defense mechanism, expressed in a reluctance to go outside their local community, limiting institutional contacts to the necessary minimum, lack of acceptance for mixed marriages, low educational aspirations, persistence of negative stereotypes and bias strengthened by the deepening difficulties of everyday life as a result of an inefficient economy. There were also conflicts that were not realized at the level of authority – new citizens, but at the level of interpersonal contacts within local communities.

Deprivation of agency, in the sense of depriving the local community of the possibility of having a real impact on the course of affairs concerning them, has also another "empirical ground." In the mid-1970s, the state decided to build a large coal power plant – the OPP – in the area without consulting the local community, thus from the very beginning, the investment was accompanied by controversy. In the first stage of the investment, the local population was against the construction due to fear of pollution and influx of strangers, which would weaken the local relationships and deepen the marginalization of local people on their own territory. The local community members protested also against their land being taken away; against the deterioration of soil due to the expected drop in groundwater levels associated with building giant blocks of the power plant; against the forced resettlement within the community of those residents whose houses were located close to the investment site; and against the discomfort related to a long-term construction of a giant building (Biela 1993; Berlińska 1995; Kokot 1988; Szmeja 1988; Woźniacki 1988). This would especially affect the village of Brzezie, populated almost entirely by non-indigenous people, which was located right next to the construction site.

As in the case of other major investments by the socialist government, so here the socialist government carried out its plan despite the local protests, although attempts were made to explain the positive effects of the investment to the population related to cheap energy, employment, or money for development of the Dobrzeń Wielki commune. From the residents' viewpoint, according to my research, these positive effects appeared only as late as in the 1990s, when the construction was already complete. Infrastructural grants started coming in, employment increased, and the commune earned a significant income. Flood prevention infrastructure was expanded, roads were laid down, and an entire residential district was built from the power plant's funds. Many companies of various sizes were created that cooperated with the plant, the local hospital was modernized and flats for doctors were built, the Communal Cultural Center started receiving considerable funds, new large schools and preschools were financed along with extra lessons for children and day-care for children and seniors, and so forth. It must be acknowledged that all this has greatly helped to improve the quality of life in the Dobrzeń Wielki commune.

The residents, living nearly literally in the shadow of the giant power plant (the stacks and cooling towers are over 200 meters high), began to see the facility as part of the familiar local environment that benefited them. Some informants even claimed that the OPP construction and the related resettlements were also positive in the end because the areas that the plant took over were legally debatable, which may have caused problems in the future. This could be considered idealization through history that enhances the effect of the familiar. It is a well-known effect of the mythicization of familiarity which is, in general, the attribution of the value of historical necessity to what is familiar, ours. In other words, the present state is seen as the result of a just historical process – "our" power plant justifies even what was perceived as bad before, when it was foreign (Czech 2009). However, because the community of Dobrzeń Wielki commune has a large share of the indigenous population, the new inhabitants of the residential district, both those who came to the commune as new settlers after the Second World War and those who arrived with the construction of the OPP, were viewed as Others – as people who had a clearly different lifestyle. The power plant, to the contrary, was gradually perceived as something familiar. However, the social bonds between indigenous population and newcomers that would create a local community through the construction of the OPP, which serves the whole community equally, were not established yet. Consequently, until recently, there had been two communities living alongside each other, with strong negative mutual stereotypes. This is an important part of what would become the backdrop for the current conflict dynamics.

Course of the Conflict

The current conflict has political, social, and ethnic aspects and develops along two opposite lines: state versus community and majority versus minority.

State vs. community. The opposition between the state authorities and the local authorities, which had been dormant since the beginning of the 1990s, has now awakened again. It should be remembered that before the Second World War most inhabitants of the commune declared more likely Polish national identity, and the German authorities carried out a widespread Germanisation campaign, perceived commonly as imposed from outside. It included changing surnames to sound German, ordering that German names be given to new-born children, changing the names of towns and villages, prohibition of learning Polish in schools, and prohibition of organizing masses in Polish (Lis 2016: 30–33). After the war, the local community suffered from being recognized by Polish authorities as a foreign element, so the local leaders of the commune have been imposed from outside, never elected from local population until the 1990s. Thus, the observation made by Stefan Nowakowski (1960: 71) in the post-war years that the German-Polish antagonism in the area was of a class nature (authority vs. local population) remained valid until the establishment of a new, realistically grassroots government in the 1990s.

Today's conflict between the state authorities and the local community is replicated within the same pattern: the state authorities, represented by the voivodeship administration, acted against the local authorities. After 1990 residents of the Dobrzeń Wielki commune have never considered their own, communal authorities as completely positive, because many people accused them of preserving privileges for a small group of indigenous residents and forming "ethnic network," to use Don Handelman's (1977: 194–196) term. However, at the same time local authorities has been a familiar power that represented the residents' empowerment. The "local community," in the sense of large we-type group with strong ties based on shared interests and needs, as well as a sense of belonging to the place one lives in, which did not develop before, has emerged during the conflict. It was being produced by multiplied signs of unity, like special songs written for the occasion and distributed among community members, posters, billboards, handmade local flags, t-shirts, and stickers with commune logo. The communal authorities, who engaged strongly in the fight against governmental representation, have become a symbol of empowerment of the whole community in the face of the political conflict with a more powerful enemy. The references to "occupation," or "partition" during the protests were not accidental, as the imbalance of power was also significant at the time. The main trigger of the protests was state authorities' reaction to result of the referendum, which they themselves proposed as a part of the consultations on the project to enlarge Opole. In the beginning of 2016, both in the city of Opole and in the Dobrzeń Wielki commune referendums were organized to see what percentage of the population supports the idea of enlarging the city at the expense of the surrounding communes. The referendum in Opole was attended by only 6 percent of eligible voters, of whom less than 3.5 percent were in favor of expanding the city's boundaries, while in the Dobrzeń Wielki commune as many as 99.7 percent of voters, with a turnout of 62 percent, voted against the enlargement of Opole. Joint protest actions started even before the state authorities ignored the obvious referendum result, but after this act, especially after the Polish government accepted enlargement plans on July 19, 2016, they have taken more drastic forms. Roadblocks or street protests in Opole gathered hundreds of people, and the hunger protest, despite attempts to discredit it in the government media, had considerable support from local residents, while building strong emotions around government decisions.[7] The commune residents gathered in hundreds every 19 each month in front of the Voivodship Office for what they called a "commemorations of the burial of democracy in the Opole region." On March 19, 2017, talks with protesters also broke down.

Perhaps the heroic connotation related to uneven forces is less important here than the issue of agency in times of crisis – the agency on the part of the consolidated community. The motto of the protests, which could be seen on almost every fence in every village of the commune, referred to this alleged community and was "The whole commune always together." The establishment of the alleged community on the immemorial timeline, by using the term "always," which is obviously not literal, although reinforces the message and refers to the quasi-grammatical opposition of the we-others ("community" vs. "others"),[8] is simultaneously clearly mythical in nature. Its ad hoc impact was finally confirmed when the actual partition of the commune took place after protests failed to bring a positive result. At that time strong divisions have re-emerged, which resulted initially in a conflict in the Communal Council, and eventually in a change of communal authorities. Furthermore, it has changed the attitude of some of the commune's inhabitants, particularly of the villages incorporated into Opole (such as Czarnowąsy), from whom it was possible to hear that the domination of the village of Dobrzeń Wielki was always to the detriment of their own village.

Moreover, tensions and the division line between local authorities and the local community was reintroduced based on the failure of struggle against the state. The failure affected common perception of the OPP

7 A detailed report on the first stages of protests is available on the website of the National Assembly of Local Authorities and Local Media, see Sejmik samorządów i mediów lokalnych 2016.

8 I use the term "quasi-grammar" instead of the structuralist term "grammar of culture" to denote the set of underlying oppositions and the mediating elements between them that provide a cognitive guide for certain societies in understanding reality. The structuralist approach suggests too much equivalence between classificatory mental processes and linguistic structures, although the very mechanism of binary ordering of reality is not questioned by modern psychology or neuroscience. Hence, the use of the term "quasi-grammar" seems more appropriate, suggesting similarity rather than dissecting the nature of the classificatory cognitive process.

itself – after incorporation of the power plant into Opole, the large industrial facility became "the stranger." The critical voices against OPP pointed out that, contrary to the "good changes" for the local community announced under Corporate Social Responsibility of the OPP (Czech 2009: 74), there is no real impact of the construction and expansion of the power plant on improving the situation on the local labor market. On the contrary, there are additional problems caused by the lowering of groundwater levels, dust and pollution associated with the presence of heavy equipment etc. "The common good," which the investment was supposed to be, is apparently becoming less common for the residents of the Dobrzeń Wielki commune.

Majority vs. minority. The unfair fight in the Dobrzeń Wielki commune has expanded with the relationship between ethnicity and state authorities. The state representatives and Opole public media used not only the existing ethnic stereotypes, but also quasi-grammar structure of the we–others relations to navigate the conflict toward majority-minority clash in the commune. Grammaticalization, which reduces the complexity of interpersonal and intergroup relationships to the "we–others" relations in the area, has a long history and precedes any national bonds or antagonisms (Sołdra-Gwiżdż 2010: 76). That is why it so easily becomes the foundation of local policies that regulate social emotions on an ad hoc basis. The German minority was supposed to serve as a prototypical other, that is, against the majority, Poles, who were supposedly backing the state. Of course, Poles in the Dobrzeń Wielki commune constitute a majority who voted against the incorporation of part of the commune into Opole, but as for the mythical figure used by the state and Opole authorities, this is irrelevant, because as semioticians of the Tartu-Moscow school claim, myth is stronger than facts (Stomma 2002: 90–91). Therefore, for many people valuing ideology over empirical facts, believing that when principles are conflated with facts, principles are truer, is the norm. Thus, Opole authorities hoped to build resentments over the existing once since post-war period when mutual stereotypes in the commune got a new solid ground. The governmental media campaigned against protests using a figure of the German-Other, the stranger who collaborates with outer, foreign forces that conspire against Poles and Poland or claiming that German minority is trying to secure their political interests with protests. However, the governmental campaign failed, because for the last several years one has witnessed an intensifying identification with the common place of residence in the commune, changing ethnic distances, and a growing feeling of "local community," regardless of whether someone is indigenous or not. For this reason, the Germans, whose involvement was meant to foster temporary political interests, have not become an antagonizing factor for the local community.

On the other hand, the category of being a "German" (or even the term "Volksdeutch," which the Opole city spokeswoman publicly used against the protesters) is clearly used by state politicians as a sign and its conventional nature has been made visible to the Dobrzeń Wielki community and recognized as a temporary political use. As a result, the category has lost its modelling power: it does not drive the conflict. It is very significant that the inscription on one of the banners during the protests read "Do not expel Poland from our hearts!" However, the use of the ethnic category initiated its presence in the temporary quasi-grammar of the conflict: the local community in Dobrzeń Wielki has clearly begun to point out the ethnic otherness of the state side of the conflict. In their view, it is represented by, as I heard several times, "the other, non-European civilization." It refers to the Romani (exemplified by the then member of the government, Patryk Jaki, one of the authors of the Opole enlargement project who is said to be of Roma origin) and the Jews (represented by the Mayor of Opole, Arkadiusz Wiśniewski), who in Polish and Silesian culture both constitute almost archetypal Others.

Conclusion

Dobrzeń Wielki is a village and a small commune inhabited by both indigenous population with strong local ties and "local identity" that dominates other identities imposed by the nation state, and newcomers, people who migrated there in a few waves, the biggest one related to the building of the OPP. There has never been a unity between those two groups until the recent decade, when there emerged an increasing number of unifying elements, such as intergroup marriages, common institutions, or common experiences with migration for work. The indigenous population had a strong sense of deprivation of agency until the early 1990s, when their representatives took over local governance. However, when the completed in 2017 process of annexation of the part of the commune by the city of Opole, including the power plant, began, this has triggered widespread public protests in the commune. They were, however, gradually suppressed, and the voice of the local people was silenced again as a few times in the past. Submitting the case to European Court of Human Rights in Strasbourg after having exhausted all formal channels in Poland helped nothing. However, the confrontation of the local community and the state revealed that there is more unity within the community than before crisis. The crisis evoked the sense of empowerment of the whole community in the face of political conflict. On the other hand, the state representatives and Opole public media tried to use ethnic stereotypes and we–others relations to navigate the conflict toward majority-minority clash, with German minority as a prototypical Other.

In short, the conflict surrounding the expansion of Opole is based on both sides on quasi-grammar that temporarily reduced the complexity of the situation to a narrow set of binary oppositions (we–others), and as such created a feeling of a presumed community among the inhabitants of Dobrzeń Wielki commune. Ethnic stereotypes, that for many years were dividing the community into local German-Silesians and Poles, had been shifted from local divisions to external ones as they started to be used by the "land-grabbing state" – "the Other." It seems that the mobilization of the community related to political pressure is weakening nowadays. However, the local community has been endowed with new signs of identity which diminished ethnic stereotypes and enriched the community with the memory of a common struggle and sacrifice. This "individual experience of collectively shared problems" (Günther 2016: 55) brings a sense of agency, and these new signs fill the local semiosphere that serves as a potential source of integration of the local community above ethnic divisions.

References

Berlińska, Danuta. "Narodowo-etniczne stosunki międzygrupowe na Śląsku Opolskim: Ciągłość i zmiana." In: *Polacy, Ślązacy, Niemcy: Studia nad stosunkami społeczno-kulturowymi na Śląsku*

Opolskim, ed. Krzysztof Frysztacki. Kraków: Universitas, 1998, pp. 33–74.

Biela, Adam. "Psychologiczne przesłanki strategii mediacyjnej w rozwiązywaniu konfliktu ekologicznego związanego z Elektrownią 'Opole'." In: *Elektrownia "Opole" a Środowisko Społeczne*, ed. Barbara Łuszczewska. Opole: Instytut Śląski, 1993, pp. 171–179.

Billig, Michael. *Banal Nationalism*. London: Sage Publications, 1995.

Choroś, Błażej and Ewa Skrabacz. "Mniejszość niemiecka w prasie regionalnej w sytuacji konfliktu: Framing i agenda medialna w ramach sporu o 'Duże Opole'." *Pogranicze : Polish Borderlands Studies* 5(3)/ 2017, pp. 161–183.

Czech, Henryk. "Zmiana postrzegania Elektrowni Opole w województwie opolskim." In: *Budowa Bloków 5 i 6 w PGE Elektrowni Opole SA – Aspekty Gospodarcze, Środowiskowe i Społeczne*, ed. Czesława Rosik-Dulewska, Grzegorz Kusza. Opole: Uniwersytet Opolski, 2009, pp. 71–90.

Frysztacki, Krzysztof. *Polacy, Ślązacy, Niemcy: Studia nad stosunkami społeczno-kulturowymi na Śląsku Opolskim*. Kraków: Universitas, 1998.

Günther, Jana. "Protest as Symbolic Politics." In: *Protest Cultures: A Companion*, ed. Kathrin Fahlenbrah, Martin Klimke, and Joachim Scharloth. New York: Berghahn Books, 2016, pp. 48–64.

Handelman, Don. "The Organization of Ethnicity." *Ethnic Groups* 1(3)/ 1977, pp. 187–200.

Jasiewicz, Joanna. "When the Past Matters: Memory Politics and Ethnic Relations in Poland." *Ethnic and Racial Studies* 38(9)/2015, pp. 1573–1590.

Kijonka, Justyna. "Migracje z Górnego Śląska do Republiki Federalnej Niemiec w latach 1970–1989, czyli między ojczyzną prywatną a ideologiczną." *Górnośląskie Studia Socjologiczne: Seria Nowa* 4/2013, pp. 29–47.

Kokot, Alojzy. "Przemiany społeczno-gospodarcze w gminie Dobrzeń Wielki pod wpływem intensywnej industrializacji." *Zeszyty Naukowe Wyższej Szkoły Inżynierskiej w Opolu* 148(21)/1988, pp. 155–166.

Lis, Michał. *Śląsk Opolski w warunkach transformacji ustrojowej państwa od 1989 roku*. Opole: Instytut Śląski, 2013.

Lis, Michał. *Mniejszość niemiecka na Śląsku Opolskim 1989–2014: Z bagażem przeszłości w realiach współczesności: Wydanie drugie poprawione*. Opole: Instytut Śląski, 2016.

Malarski, Stanisław. "Ewolucja zmian postaw społecznych i opinii wobec Elektrowni 'Opole.'" *Śląsk Opolski* 2/1995, pp. 3–9.

Nowakowski, Stefan. *Przeobrażenia społeczne wsi opolskiej*. Poznań: Instytut Zachodni, 1960.

Nycz, Edward. "Współczesne identyfikacje mieszkańców pogranicza etniczno-kulturowego." *Śląsk Opolski* (2–3)/2010, pp. 47–60.

Olszewska, Anna. *Wieś uprzemysłowiona: Studium społeczności lokalnej w powiecie opolskim*. Wrocław: Zakład Narodowy im. Ossolińskich, 1969.

Ossowski, Stanisław. "Zagadnienie więzi regionalnej i więzi narodowej na Śląsku Opolskim." *Przegląd Socjologiczny* 9(1–4)/1947, pp. 73–124.

Rauziński, Robert. "Społeczno-demograficzne problemy Dobrzenia Wielkiego w okresie budowy Elektrowni 'Opole.'" *Śląsk Opolski* 2/ 1995, pp. 10–12.

Simonides, Dorota. "Śląskie kłopoty z tożsamością." In: *Nadciągają Ślązacy: Czy istnieje narodowość śląska?*, ed. Lech Nijakowski. Warszawa: Scholar, 2004, pp. 157–164.

Sejmik samorządów i mediów lokalnych. *Komunikat z XX ogólnopolskiego sejmiku samorządów i mediów lokalnych*. 2016. http://dobrzenwielki.pl/2384/xx-ogolnopolski-sejmik-samorzadow-i-mediow-lokalnych.html (23 Sept. 2017).

Sołdra-Gwiżdż, Teresa. *Socjologia wobec Śląska – jedność czy wielość?* Opole: Instytut Śląski, 2010.

Stomma, Ludwik. *Antropologia kultury wsi polskiej XIX wieku oraz wybrane eseje*. Łódź: Piotr Dopierała, 2002.

Szmeja, Maria. "Przemiany społeczności gminy Dobrzeń Wielki pod wpływem budowy elektrowni." *Zeszyty Naukowe Wyższej Szkoły Inżynierskiej w Opolu* 148(21)/1988, pp. 127–134.

Szmeja, Maria. *Starzy i nowi mieszkańcy Opolszczyzny*. Opole: Instytut Śląski, 1997.

Szmeja, Maria. *Niemcy? Polacy? Ślązacy! Rodzimi mieszkańcy Opolszczyzny w świetle analiz socjologicznych*. Kraków: Universitas, 2000.

Tambiah, Stanley J. "The Nation-State in Crisis and the Rise of Ethnonationalism." In: *The Politics of Difference: Ethnic Premises in a World of Power*, ed. Edwin N. Wilmsen, Patrick McAllister. Chicago: University of Chicago Press, 1996, pp. 124–143.

Turner, Victor. *Dramas, Fields, and Metaphors: Symbolic Action in Human Society*. Ithaca: Cornell University Press, 1975.

Woźniacki, Janusz. "System wartości mieszkańców Dobrzenia Wielkiego a postrzeganie budowy elektrowni i zmian przez nią wywołanych." *Zeszyty Naukowe Wyższej Szkoły Inżynierskiej w Opolu* 148(21)?1988, pp. 135–154.

Monika Baer[1]

Affective Togetherness: Emotional Dynamics in/of the Field of the Political

Abstract: This chapter aims to analyze emotional dynamics in/of the field of the political that emerged due to a planned takeover of a part of Dobrzeń Wielki commune by a neighboring city of Opole in Opole Silesia in southwestern Poland. Drawing on an ethnographic detail, it investigates changing forms of affective togetherness that originated from and gave way to grassroots social protests. In particular, the chapter explores "ethics of probability" and "ethics of possibility" connected to the anticipation of an uncertain future that have shaped the discussed social/political processes and phenomena.

Key words: affective togetherness, anticipations, emotions, the political, social protests.

Emotions, the Political, and Anticipations

The issue of emotions has been the subject of reflection in social sciences and humanities from the very beginning of shaping their contemporary forms.[2] However, the consciously articulated "turn" towards this subject in social and cultural anthropology is usually associated primarily with the 1980s and the names of authors such as Michelle Rosaldo (1980), Lila Abu-Lughod (1986) or Catherine Lutz (1988). Recent decades have brought a wide spectrum of postulates and discussions about what emotions are, as well as how they should be analyzed (e.g. Lutz 2017; Svašek 2002; Skoggard, Waterston 2015). Regardless of specific theoretical and

---

1 Department of Ethnology and Cultural Anthropology, University of Wroclaw, monika.baer@uwr.edu.pl, ORCID: 0002-2415-1060.

2 Being aware that emotions, feelings, or affects are variously understood in social sciences and humanities, and frequently assigned contrasting meanings (see e.g. Ahmed 2014: 205–211; Skoggard, Waterston 2015), in this chapter I use the first category as an umbrella term that pertains mostly to political, social and relational dimensions of these entities, but leaves aside the biocultural matters (more on this issue see Lutz 2017).

methodological assumptions underlying the ongoing debates, one of the elements that binds anthropological analyses in this area is a focus on their agency in the process of (re)creating realities (e.g. Lutz, Abu-Lughod 1990; Svašek 2008b; Ahmed 2014).

In line with the above reasoning, set by such classics as *Language and the Politics of Emotion* (Lutz, Abu-Lughod 1990), emotions can be seen in terms of discursive practices entangled and embedded in wider relations of power. They are thereby closely related to "politics" and "political." Chantal Mouffe (2005: 9) defines the political as "the dimension of antagonism," which is "constitutive of human societies." In contrast, she characterizes the politics as denoting "a set of practices and institutions through which order and organization is created, organizing human existence in the context of conflictuality provided by the political." The political means therefore "the wider field of contingency and struggle that exceeds established regimes of politics" (Dzenovska, De Genova 2018: 3). As Maruška Svašek (2008a) points out, although politics is conventionally considered as rational decision-making, it is obvious that an inherent aspect of political processes is their emotional dimension. At the same time, the emotions themselves are also strongly politicized. Since their constitutive agency in socio-cultural processes is related to the distribution of power, many affective phenomena concern domination, resistance, and cooperation. In this context, emotions thus form a dialectical bridge between what is "individual" and what is "social:" "as positioned, socially embedded, thinking and feeling individuals," people are "politically motivated and manipulated by hope, disappointment, joy and fear" (Svašek 2008a: 7).

Emotions can therefore be apprehended as "discursive public forms" (Appadurai 1990: 93) through which not only the capillary power of governmentality in Michel Foucault's sense operates (see e.g. Rose et al. 2006), but also practices of resistance pressing on subjects legally and/or socially legitimized in the field of power (Svašek 2008a: 7; Merry 1995: 16–17; see also Appadurai 2016). The emerging "political" becomes an arena of forging more or less stable affective togetherness of different temporal and spatial scales (Dzenovska, De Genova 2018). In this sense, the emotionally charged discourses of subjects less privileged in the field of power develop into the "weapons of the weak" (Scott 1985). They serve to build a sense of individual and/or collective agency and symbolic equality towards actors more privileged within objectified social structures. In the sphere of the political, emotions thus not only have a pragmatic dimension, but function also as a communicative performance (Abu-Lughod, Lutz 1990).

Such affective practices in the field of the political frequently relate to hope that "hold[s] the promise of overcoming the oppressive present and the dystopian futures inherent in it" (Dzenovska, De Genova 2018: 3). It is therefore unsurprising that the "affective turn" is associated with "the rise of regimes of anticipation" (Lutz 2017: 187–188). At least since the early twenty-first century, anthropological discussions on emotions have been accompanied by reflections on the future and related images, but most of all on uncertainty (e.g. Akama et al. 2018; Appadurai 2013; Salazar et al. 2017; Samimian-Darash, Rabinow 2015). In essence, it is uncertainty that merge the discursive practices of the future with discursive practices of emotions. Yoko Akama, Sarah Pink, and Shanti Sumartojo (2018) claim that uncertainty is an increasingly significant feature of the present – it is not only "a way of being," but also an essential cognitive strategy. Recognizing in a sense the omnipresence of uncertainty, the authors emphasize that it is worth recognizing its potential. Similarly to ethnographic practice understood as a device for "generating surprises" (Fortun 2012: 451), the uncertainty of the present allows to see it as constantly emerging, where the ongoing reconfiguration of things and processes does not permit to define anything for sure. In such a perspective, uncertainty ceases to be inevitably risky or dangerous, and becomes inevitably creative. Thus, it opens a space for the politics and ethics of hope.

Just like other emotions, hope is being politicized on the one hand, whereas on the other, it remains embedded within and launches specific norms, convictions, and values that pertain to morality. Arjun Appadurai (2013: 293, 295) believes that "hope is the political counterpart of the work of the imagination ... [f]or it is only through some sort of politics of hope that any society or group can envisage a journey to desirable change in the state of things." As a result, any anticipation of future combines the "ethics of probability" and the "ethics of possibility." While the former focuses on risks and dangers and subsequent management and surveillance, the latter provides "ways of thinking, feeling, and acting that increase the horizons of hope." The "ethics of possibility" allows thereby to aspire to and act for "good life." It is a "tectonic struggle between these two ethics" that, according to Appadurai, lies at the basis of processes constitutive for the global present, including the contradictions inherent in it.

In this chapter I adapt the above theoretical framework to smaller-scale issues. To this effect, I look at how the clash of the two above-mentioned ethics have marked emotionally charged discursive practices connected to the anticipation of an uncertain future, which emerged from a plan to include a part of the Dobrzeń Wielki commune within the administrative boundaries of the city of Opole in Opole Silesia in southwestern Poland.[3] It is not my aim to present in detail all the facts or to thoroughly describe the entire phenomena caused by this event. I intent rather to map shock, anger, outrage, fear, resentment, resignation, skepticism, hope, enthusiasm, or faith which brought affective togetherness among residents protesting against the commune's division and related developments. In the resultant field of the political, the discussed emotions as well as their particular "addressees" changed significantly over time. It is precisely these emotional dynamics that are the focus of this analysis.

Fieldwork

The analyzed material was collected in the course of ethnographic field research conducted between February 2015 and November 2018 as a part of team research project concerning the cultural, social, political, and economic processes which were the result of and the context for relations between the Opole Power Plant (OPP) and the residents of the Dobrzeń Wielki commune. Those processes were analyzed first and foremost in the light of the ongoing expansion of the plant's fifth and sixth block, which at the time was one of the largest investments in the European energy

3 The expansion of the city of Opole did not concern solely the Dobrzeń Wielki commune, but also other neighboring communes. However, in this chapter I focus on events related only to this one specific case.

sector.[4] In this context, together with Ewa Kruk, we were exploring gendered aspects of late industrialism. We were primarily interested in the career paths of women connected with an industrial workplace, in the social activities of women in the commune, and in migration experience of women. However, the research situation changed dramatically when, at the end of 2015, the plan to include several villages, and the OPP itself, within the administrative boundaries of the city of Opole was exposed. Therefore, even though we did not give up on our previous interests, we could not ignore the issues that became the main subject of extremely emotional conversations with the inhabitants of Dobrzeń Wielki and other villages. As Lutz (2017: 181) notes, emotions can be thought of as "devices for identifying what comes to matter to people in diverse historical, cultural, and political contexts," both individually and collectively. They thus become signposts revealing how various types of changes affect people connected by a certain sense of sharing a cause, place and/or time.

The point of departure for analyzing affective togetherness emerging in the context of at first anticipated, and then the actual division of the commune, involved women engaged in social activities related to the Communal Cultural Center (CCC). At the time of research, the center remained one of the most important initiators and/or supporters of cultural and social events in the commune. The research participants included persons of differentiated sociodemographic profiles, but united by their commitment to various social initiatives. These comprised educational forum focused on family issues, an association working for local community, a vocal ensemble, and a sporting group. The research took the form of both open, in-depth, partially structured, and structured interviews, but also informal chats with members of the above groups and with people more

4 The project *Conflict, Tension and Cooperation: A Case Study of Mutual Impact between the Opole Power Plant and the Community of Dobrzeń Wielki* was implemented from August 2014 to January 2019 at the University of Wroclaw with Petr Skalník as the Principal Investigator. It was financed by the National Science Center, grant number 2013/11/b/HS3/03895.

or less directly related to their activities.[5] They were supported by participatory and non-participatory observation during their meetings and activities and during local events important for our interlocutors, but also for residents of the commune in general. These classic ethnographic methods have been supplemented with an analysis of public discourses, primarily in the form of press publications, Internet publications and statements, and other information materials (more on this issue see Baer 2018).

It is therefore specifically "situated knowledge" (in Donna Haraway's sense, 1988), reflecting precise spatial, cultural, social, and political locations, which I analyze here. However, because the late modernity is a product of many technical, biophysical, cultural, political, legal or economic nested systems of various scales, involved in multiple and complex relations, such context implies a multitude of interactions and makes keeping the analyzed problems "in place" impossible. The emerging phenomena need to be followed through spaces and social groups (see e.g. Falzon 2009; Fortun 2012). The discursive practices of particular group of socially active women led me thus in numerous "real" and "virtual" directions within administrative territory of the commune and beyond. By participating in meetings and demonstrations, listening to and/or talking to those residents of the commune who were not indifferent to "annexation,"[6] reading publications and posts on social media, I was able to look at the analyzed issues from a much broader perspective. Effectively, the affective togetherness in question was strictly related to a wider discursive field that emerged from the commune's division than the main interviewees' narratives.

Doxa

Our interlocutors reported that they had learnt about the planned division from the media on November 23, 2015: "The head of the commune found out from the paper around 4 p.m., and at 5 p.m. it was already

---

5 In this context, we conducted thirty-two formal interviews. The first category consisted of eighteen persons with the key interlocutors met repeatedly on subsequent field trips. The second category contained five persons.

6 Unacknowledged quotations originate from fieldwork material and have been translated into English by the author.

online ... It came as a shock to everyone." That shock resulted in actions which in the following years would shape the field of the political, whose highest intensity was the end of 2015, 2016, and the beginning of 2017, that is, the period in which the division remained an anticipation, not yet a fact. During that time, the discursive practices concerning the planned overtaking of a part of the Dobrzeń Wielki commune by the city of Opole oscillated around a deep sense of harm and a conviction that "it's already done" and a hope that perhaps through social protests, legal procedures, and other political strategies the division could be prevented. The resulting affective togetherness was linked by the reproduction of certain *doxa* in a sense of Pierre Bourdieu (see e.g. Jacyno 1997: 55–58). It was formed by the assumed causes and anticipated effects of the commune's division, where the above-mentioned "ethics of probability" constantly clashed with "ethics of possibility." This *doxa* was first and foremost created and distributed in local discourses of authority – at the level of communal and provincial institutions, by local journalists, representatives of the academia, or social protest leaders. For some time, those discourses constituted an indisputable narrative referenced (although in slightly differing versions) in statements of various scales. They could be found, for instance, in the national media which supported the protest against the planned partition. However, most of all they were present in accounts of ordinary people living in the commune, emotionally connected with it, or simply rooting for "Dobrzeń" against "Opole" for political and ethical reasons. Therefore, the *doxa* was revealing the most socially relevant issues at that time.

Among its essential elements were the financial matters. However, all transactions and other economic phenomena, including the very category of "money," carry diverse moral, symbolic, social, and political messages (see e.g. Bloch, Parry 1989). As Alaina Lemon (1998: 22) notes, "[t]he calibration of things on like scales, the abstraction of values, is one of the supposed contributions of money to civilization ... While most cultural anthropologists ... would argue that values, whether converted into monetary amounts or not, are refracted through 'cultures,' a habit lingers to consider money as itself an abstraction. However, while money does work to abstract some values, it not only does so in culturally specific ways but also works to concretize other values." In this sense, money becomes a window which allows an insight into non-economic aspects of the analyzed world (Lutz 2017: 184–185).

In the discussed period, one of the main adversaries of "Dobrzeń" was the Mayor of Opole. From the very beginning, the will to take over a part of the commune was interpreted as his will to take over the taxes from the OPP and other large companies in its vicinity: "This is about money, because [he] needs money ... There are leaflets already, there was something like this in Opole: what you can gain from the annexation, and there was this graph showing how many millions will go into the municipal budget." Deprived of two-thirds of its previous budget, the commune was presented as inviable: "It's as if you took away someone's lungs and kidneys and told them to live on, while they don't even have a say in it." In this context, there was information about the need to abandon planned road repairs or the construction of a new sewage treatment plant, about the closure of well-equipped communal schools, about hundreds of people losing their jobs, about the collapse of the CCC, and, consequently, about the disappearance of any activities addressed to residents, including a wide range of activities for children and the elderly.

Similar emotions could be heard in the discourses of our interlocutors engaged in social activities within the commune. They emphasized that "Opole's" conviction that "in Dobrzeń they only fight for money" was very hurtful. What they were fighting for was to maintain the existing "good life." According to the research participants, the future was looking dark, marked by a fear verging on certainty that "everything will disappear" and "we will have nothing left." Their narratives differed slightly depending on the location of particular types of activity. People living in the villages which were to be incorporated into Opole remained convinced that the main costs of changing the city boundaries would be borne by the inhabitants of the annexed areas. In the case of social activity, the difference was associated with lower subsidies and the inability to apply for funding addressed to rural areas. However, activists whose initiatives were to stay in the reduced commune were equally pessimistic about their actions: "I'm scared, because I have ambitions, dreams, and plans, and I'm scared that ... they are all in vain ... The head of the commune has told me that if there's no income, there might be no money for it."

Situated Togetherness

Sarah Ahmed (2014: 10) points out that "emotions are not simply something 'I' or 'we' have. Rather, it is through emotions, or how we respond to objects and others, that surfaces or boundaries are made: the 'I' and the 'we' are shaped by, and even take the shape of, contact with others." Consequently, the affective togetherness emerging from the planned partition of the commune involved various configurations of the difference between "Dobrzeń" and "Opole." One of them activated a nationalistic thread. Even though most of Dobrzenians, according to our interlocutors, "do not have much in common with the Germans," they were "being called Germans" by the Mayor of Opole. He was reported to stress that it was the "German minority" who were protesting. In the communal discourses of authority such strategies were interpreted as "Opole rhetoric," which the municipality invoked for the use of "Warsaw," trying to turn an economic conflict into a national conflict, the one that the ruling party itself creates for political purposes. Opposing the narrative on the "German minority that does not want to lose their positions," formal and informal leaders of the protest repeatedly emphasized that they brought together people "with different political and cultural views." At the same time, it was the violation of the rights of the national minority that became one of the important premises with which the commune authorities tried to counteract its division with the use of legal tools.

However, conceiving the difference between "Dobrzeń" and "Opole" was not limited to the nationalistic issue, but it also referred to a broader question of values connected with some local ideas of Silesianity. Honesty, diligence or thriftiness of the Silesians were contrasted with the lack of respect for the Silesian system of values on the part of Opole authorities: "It's just done without thinking, nobody cares what's going to happen to another person, what the outcome will be for other people. It's only important that my needs are met. Terribly selfish. … Had the mayor been fair about this, had he paid attention to other people … there would be none of this discord, this division." The discourses disseminated in Opole, stating that the necessity to take away money from the commune resulted from its inability to manage it, were considered particularly unfair with regard to local values. In this context, the infrastructural situation in the villages of Dobrzeń Wielki commune was often compared with the situation of underinvested villages attached to Opole in earlier years: "Our village is really wonderful ..., streetlights, sidewalks, everything. ... Here, these commune authorities work as if they owned it." Investments in sports, education and language courses, kindergartens, and numerous subsidies for the residents were also indicated, as well as the transparency of the management of the commune, where "everyone knows everyone and everything."

The majority of research participants, even before the issue of the commune's division appeared, stressed its specificity resulting from a significant flow of "power plant money." It was with the wealth of the commune that the interlocutors explained, at least partially, the developing social activities of women: if someone had a good idea and came with a proposal to the commune authorities, they received funding. Nonetheless, bearing in mind the prospect of taking over taxes from the power plant by the city of Opole, it began to be emphasized that this wealth was a relatively new phenomenon which involved many non-economic costs: "The Dobrzeń Wielki commune has had money only for twenty years, previously it was the poorest commune in the district. It was a rural commune, there was nothing here until the power plant started. And there's a lot of catching up. True, we have many more things, ... [but] there are also inconveniences. And they are more serious than in the neighboring communes. So people deserve something for that, some compensation."

The anticipated destabilization of the "good life in a rich commune" changed the positioning of the OPP in the local social imaginary. Previously treated as an entity that fit "naturally" into the landscape of the commune but did not play an important role in its life (Baer 2018: 183–184), it now became the axis organizing discursive practices built around variously defined "loss." Appadurai (2013: 287–288) indicates that in producing togetherness, the essential role is played by the imagination understood as a collective practice. Consequently, the personal archives of memories of ordinary people were not really about the past but became the point of departure for negotiating and shaping the future. Such archives were thus often referred to in emotionally charged statements against the takeover of the power plant: "[G]randparents had to give up their lands, nobody asked any questions, it was practically for free. ... Because they are building here.

... And now they're gonna say: 'Why does it bother them so much?', right? It's just so ... like a slap in the face, you know." There was also the issue of "unfair" access to work in the power plant both back in the 1990s when it started to operate, and during its current enlargement: work was provided to the migrants from other parts of Poland, and the indigenous people were forced to migrate abroad for work.

The planned division of the commune also triggered new emotions related to the ongoing expansion of the OPP. While earlier its impact on the life of the commune was seen primarily through the prism of the large number of workers in local stores, in the following years other issues began to be discussed. Previously absent concerns were expressed about the consequences of the power plant itself and the current enlargement on the health of the residents of the commune, especially children, first and foremost in the context of the growing number of allergies. It was stressed that the inhabitants of the commune would still be exposed to negative environmental effects resulting from the location of the power plant, while the profits would be generated by "Opole:" "In Opole people seem to think that we're only taking advantage of the situation and we have such a cool life, because we have the power plant and some money. But nobody sees that everybody has this power plant right outside their house, and there's so many cars, everyone drives there. It's not like there are no consequences." The once nonexistent disappointment was also expressed that the ongoing expansion did not bring the expected financial profits for the residents of the commune. In addition to the above-mentioned issue of employing mainly companies and people "from outside," more often complaints were also made about the economic unprofitability of investments made in rooms for rent or in catering activities addressed to people working on the extension.

Citizenship

The majority of our interlocutors were critical towards persons who passively waited for the situation to develop and/or claimed that the division of the commune would not change anything for them. According to dominant narrative within the discussed field of the political, indifference was typical of "Opole," not "Dobrzeń:" while "people don't talk about anything else in Dobrzeń," in Opole very often they do not even know about the planned "annexation." The passivity of some of the commune's residents also problematized the sense of togetherness built around the issue of civil society and self-governance. Especially persons involved in local political activity emphasized that the planned division of the commune was an "attack against self-government:" "that's what self-governments were created for, so that the communes could manage that money, they know the needs." On the other hand, ordinary people appealed more to the broader concept of citizenship: "We might be going through such grieving since January as if we had lost a loved one. ... It had been decided for us and we're just not feeling good about it. ... People simply want to have some say in deciding about themselves, about the country, too. Not just this little homeland."

The very idea of dividing the commune was also sometimes interpreted as a purposeful strategy of destroying the affective togetherness of the residents of the Opole voivodeship, whose liquidation was being planned on a central level: "There are a lot of people living here who used to protest when [the government] many years ago wanted to divide [the Opole voivodeship]. They wouldn't go anywhere now. Someone is stealing from me and I'm supposed to protest for them? ... There is no Opole voivodeship as such anymore, there's Opole and there's us." It was the sense of civic belonging to the commune as the antithesis of "Opole" that was both the cause and the result of involvement in grassroots social protests, which from the end of 2015 became one of the most important areas for the emergence of affective togetherness. Recalling the protest actions in that first period in retrospect, our interlocutors stressed that "for the first time, people united and acted together." This sense of unity found its symbolic expression in, among others, the anthem of the commune composed especially for the purpose of the protests.

The first protests were organized in the commune itself and took the form of demonstrations in public spaces and roadblocks. The cyclical demonstrations quickly moved to Opole, and later also to Warsaw. The research participants emphasized that the protests at the beginning had the character of a "levy en masse" in which women were particularly visible, perhaps due to the traditions of their social activities. The attitude to the demonstrations in the first months after the announcement of the division plans was reflected in the statement of one of them: "I don't like such things, but sometimes you gotta do what you gotta do." The feeling of threat and anticipation of loss generated anger, which made the residents feel convinced that it was necessary to take public actions (see also Svašek 2008a: 13). Although all interlocutors insisted that they were involved in the protests as private individuals, structures related to social activities were certainly helpful, such as in the case of the preparation of banners:

> In the first week, I have a sewing group, we brought all the sewing machines, people brought theirs, it's like a regular manufacture, people were so upset. Mrs. [X] ... got us some fabric for free, and so: one person was cutting, another one was cutting smaller pieces, 12 women were sewing, a boy was carrying blank ones to the printing house, came back with printed flags, took another load of blanks, and men were putting the flags up on sticks. It was just a joint action.

However, from the very beginning, emotional and practical involvement in the protests was accompanied by the conviction that these manifestations of citizenship were solely a communicative performance: "It's just hurtful, because people over here have nothing to say. ... They protest, scream, buy some t-shirts, banners, flags, everything, and it's not working." This feeling intensified over time, especially when in mid-2016 there appeared – according to inhabitants of the commune – political pressure on the national media, which stopped reporting the protest. The most often recalled example was the manifestation during the Fifty-Third National Festival of Polish Song in Opole, which consisted of 2,000–3,000 people and was completely ignored by the national media. On the other hand, the local Opole media were mostly accused of dishonesty. In this situation, in the opinion of our interlocutors, the only reliable source of information were communal media and social media.

Parallel to the growing resentment over the suppression of the protest's visibility, and thus its political impact, discourses about other politically motivated threats began to emerge. Some of them were connected with the intensification of actions by law enforcement agencies directed against informal leaders of the protest. That kind of fears was also reflected in the discourses of ordinary people who talked during demonstrations about undercover policemen taking pictures of them or about wiretapping the people most actively involved in the protest. All this, combined with the above-mentioned attack on self-governance or questioning the right of citizens to self-determination, triggered a discourse about a "return to communism" not only at the local but also national level. The signing of the decision on the division of the commune by the Prime Minister on July 19, 2016 was commemorated with monthly demonstrations in Opole organized under the slogan "burial of democracy in the Opole region."

Discourses of Hope

Considering that anticipations marked by uncertainty usually combine "ethics of probability" with "ethics of possibility," declarations that protest "will do nothing," were still accompanied by various discourses of hope. Those with the greatest social impact were related to the aid that the commune hoped to obtain from entities located at subsequent levels of political structures. Initially, expectations were associated with the Opole voivode as the authority responsible for launching (at the request of Opole municipality) the process of changing the city borders. It was said that "he has not made the decision yet, and personally he was against;" that he would take into consideration the interests of the commune; or that he was impressed by the 5,000 signatures under a petition against the expansion of Opole. To the indignation of the commune's residents, the voivode, however, sent the application to the Council of Ministers and wrote in it that the interest in the whole matter in the attached villages was negligible. It was then that hopes began to be tied with the national level. On the one hand, they concerned the Ombudsman, who supported the actions of the Dobrzeń Wielki commune. On the other hand, they also counted on the government:

> They had no idea, how could they. There's nothing on the television, nothing on the radio. There's no information anywhere and they receive an application that people are content, and they want the annexation. ... I've recently heard that some things are slowly changing in the government, that they are realizing people just don't want that.

In this context, it was repeated that "nothing's set in stone yet;" the Mayor of Opole "hasn't got a deal;" and the national authorities were not expecting protests on such a scale. The vertical mobility of discourses of hope related to the political sphere was not weakened by the fact that the application was approved by the Prime Minister, although it caused the ruling party to join the group of adversaries of "Dobrzeń." There were attempts to get the President of the Republic of Poland, as well as European politicians, interested in the cause of "Dobrzeń." In this context, the support of the German chancellor visiting Poland and the presentation of the issue of the expansion of Opole to the European Parliament were mentioned.

Mark Goodale (2017) convincingly shows that in the late modernity the law offers instruments for individual and collective agency. It not only serves to constitute social orders, but also provides tools of resistance and thus assumes a form of "politics by other means" (Wilson 2007: 351–355). Consequently, a large part of discourses of hope were also related to legal actions taken at local, national, and European level. In this context, there were stories about the actions of the head of the commune who would "catch out" the Mayor of Opole with the help of lawyers, or about "letters" sent to Warsaw. There were also rumors that "the head of the commune had been promised" that a complaint about the infringement of right of a national minority directed to the European Court of Human Rights in Strasbourg would be "given a priority." Hopes for a dispute to be resolved by means of legal means collapsed when the Constitutional Tribunal (the constitutional court of Poland) published a position unfavorable for the commune in February 2017. Although many people believed that it would be considered positively, the complaint regarding formal flaws in the application to change the borders of Opole, violation of the interests of commune and unequal treatment of citizens, including violation of the rights of national minorities, was dismissed.

Reconfigurations of Affective Togetherness

The last socially significant spurt of the protest, which was to draw the attention of the national authorities to the commune division, was the hunger protest. It started spontaneously on the second day of Christmas 2016, after the Christmas carols concert in the CCC. Our interlocutors presented it as a grassroots initiative of residents who believed until the very last moment that the intervention of the Prime Minister would block the division of the commune. However, instead of supporting them, "the Prime Minister told us to quiet down." After some time, this initiative had, according to the participants of the protest, the desired effect: the nationwide media, as well as politicians at the national level, again became interested in the protest in "Dobrzeń:" "Warsaw showed up ... on the seventeenth day. And so we made it." The hunger protest led to the initiation of formal mediation between the authorities of the diminished commune and the authorities of Opole. However, most of the people we spoke to did not attach any serious hopes to those talks. Rather, they treated them as a strategy on the part of the national authorities, aiming at extinguishing social unrest: "[The Minister of the Interior and Administration] obliged our voivode ... to mediate, so that the two local governments could get along with each other ... [so that] people would not riot, starve, protest."

The above statement from mid-February 2017 was a sign of cracks in the existing *doxa*. When the division of the commune from an anticipated future became the experienced present, many residents (both those who remained within its borders and those who found themselves in Opole) gradually began to adapt to the new circumstances. As a result, the emotionally charged discourses of authority and those of ordinary people became increasingly divergent. Previous forms of affective togetherness were becoming fragmented, setting in motion the poles of the field of the political: former allies now became adversaries. In essence, even though numerous inhabitants as well as the authorities of the commune still perceived the partition as a disaster, the so far unproblematized assumptions and beliefs related to this event, which formed the hitherto *doxa*, were turned into *orthodoxa* striving to keep the structure of the field of the political untouched. Such a stance was criticized within emerging *heterodoxa* aimed at changing the nature of the discussed field (more on this type of dynamics see Jacyno 1997: 55–58).

In fact, the attitude of the commune residents to the ongoing protest began to shift already in mid-2016. While the discourses of authority assumed that approval of the expansion of Opole by the Prime Minister would cause its escalation, because "emotions would reach their zenith," our interlocutors at the same time claimed that "there is less and less of this spirit in the nation." It was then that critical voices began to appear regarding the forms that the protest took. There was talk of the "carnival" and not truly "revolutionary" character of the demonstrations in Opole, due to the majorettes and the communal brass band taking part in them, or the "appropriation" of the protest by people who impose its specific models, such as roadblocks: "I don't even want to hear it anymore when I hear about yet another protest. I think some of those are pointless. Why block the roads? What's the point? Our people ... are stuck in traffic since 5 a.m. Or they set off to work at 5 a.m., so that they can make it by 8 a.m." In general, more and more often one could hear that "people don't feel like protesting any more" and that they were tired. These discourses grew stronger as reflected in the less and less interest in the protest against the division of the commune in the following years.

From 2017, the above critical voices began to be associated with criticism toward the formal animators of the fight against the division, that is, the commune authorities. Initially, they were the result of disappointment with the lack of effectiveness of more than a year of joint efforts:

> Had there been a hunger strike from the beginning, had there been decent protests, it would look different. ... Why is it that when miners are protesting ... then everything's done? Because they yell. Because people are afraid of them. ... And here sixteen days of hunger strike and nothing? ... Anyhow, they treated us like that because of the head of the commune, because he would quiet it all down and say: more calmly and more calmly.

However, because trusting is "an emotionally ambiguous project, in which feelings of safety that are inherent in trusting relationships are always threatened by the possibility of insincerity and betrayal" (Svašek 2008a: 14), those moods triggered or highlighted the previously existing conflicts on methods of managing the commune. Pressing on the hitherto unproblematized *doxa*, the *heterodoxa* contributed to the emergence of affective togetherness whose criticism was no longer directed mainly at the authorities of Opole or the ruling party, but at the commune authorities. The discursive practices took the form of a communicative performance, in which an important role was played by "gossip" – a political tool of people who felt that they had no influence on what was happening around them. Nonetheless, as the future showed, their embedding in the local field of the political caused that in that particular case emotions had a measurable impact on shaping the future (see also Müller 2008).

As before, most of the statements seemingly concerned economic issues. Discourses related to the lack of efficiency or transparency in the management of the commune, which evolved around "malpractices," attributed them, however, not so much to a financial nature, but to an ethical one: "We had such millions ... and nobody knows what happened with that money. People are opening their eyes now, because once we saw the budget everyone started asking where that money was. Now it's all coming to light." In this context, high salaries, irregularities in the employment structure, and other problems related to the functioning of communal institutions were discussed in detail. There was talk of "strange arrangements" where the policy of "supporting local entrepreneurs" often took the form of an expensive "monopoly." It was also emphasized that the savings related to the reduced communal budget were connected with the reduction of the earnings of all people employed in commune structures, except for the highest levels of the Commune Office.

Investments in infrastructure, which had previously been the subject of pride of the inhabitants of the commune, began to be interpreted differently. Now they became a contribution to discussing the ineptitude of local authorities. The underinvested peripheral districts of Opole as a point of reference were replaced in residents' stories by neighboring communes, which, having much smaller budgets, were able to carry out what the Dobrzeń Wielki commune could not: "No matter how you look at it, the [Y] commune ... was somehow able to renovate the entire CCC and provide activities for children. And they could do the sidewalks, and they somehow manage." It was stressed that the authorities of "Dobrzeń," used to "the power plant money," were never interested in alternative sources of funding, such as EU funds, owing to which much poorer communes were "blossoming." The anticipations expressed in the discourses of authority (still in the first months of 2018) that the division of the commune would make it inviable in the future, became interpreted in terms of an "affective economy," where emotions serve as circulating capital that produces collective subjects (Ahmed 2014: 44–46). The announced necessity to close communal schools or the CCC ceased to be treated as a real threat but began to be seen rather as a kind of "affective investment" (Svašek 2008a: 19): "a propaganda" aiming to "show that we are martyrs" and to "trigger people."

Toward Alternative Futures

The above reconfiguration meant that, contrary to the beliefs maintained by the discourses of authority that in the villages taken over by Opole "nobody takes into account that ... the situation [of division] will last longer," according to our interlocutors from these villages, most of their residents were not particularly interested in returning to the commune. It seems the primal forms of affective togetherness were caused first of all by the hope for a shape of the future different from the one anticipated, which was anchored in the very process of action (see Dzenovska, De Genova 2018: 5). As the probable became certain, the impact of earlier forms of "ethics of possibility" clearly diminished. In the first months of 2017, it seemed that ordinary people were occupied with the practical aspects of everyday life much more than broader issues of a political nature. The residents of the commune, located on both sides of the new border, talked mainly about higher bills or taxes, about the elimination of various commune subsidies, or about the costs and problems related to the exchange of documents, the change of car registration plates or the re-registration of companies. However, those discourses were gradually complemented with new aspirations towards "a good life." Although the research participants admitted that the division of the commune "cost them money," they emphasized that locally "they live the same way as before" and "try to stick together." Contrary to expectations from the beginning of 2017, when the feeling of "suspension" still prevailed, it also turned out that those who wanted to become socially involved could still do it, even if sometimes in a slightly different manner than before (Baer 2018: 196–198).

Until the end of 2018, new opportunities emerging from the division of the commune were undoubtedly to a greater extent attainable in villages attached to Opole. People wishing to act for the benefit of their communities found spaces for this type of activity, for example, in district councils elected in autumn 2017. New structures and/or municipal sources of funding provided residents with access to most of the events that previously defined their local "ways of being." The peculiar sense of continuity thus maintained was supplemented by new amenities, such as city bus transport or the Opole Senior Citizen Card, which entitled the holder to discounts. However, in the discourses of local activists who had been involved in the social life of the commune for many years, nostalgia for what was, "what the commune gave," echoed. Since their affective togetherness with "Dobrzeń" was marked by the lack of trust in "Opole" formed during the protest, they stressed that financial investments in new districts were only temporary tools to finally calm down rebellious moods and to "shut the mouths" of those criticizing the city authorities.

At first glance, the situation in the diminished commune was much worse, not only due to much smaller financial resources, but also due to conflicts that the division of the commune revealed or launched. However, even though, according to our interlocutors, the commune became "somewhat lifeless" and "sad," there was no talk of a "God knows what kind of tragedy." Hence, here as well, new versions of the "ethics of possibility" emerged, problematizing the earlier "ethics of probability." In spite of not the best moods, the research participants emphasized that they are "coping," hoping that the future will bring "a change for the better." The source of this change was not to be the struggle to restore the previous boundaries of the commune, but the ability to adapt to the new circumstances. As one of them said, "when one gate closes, a new one has to open in its place. ... We just need to look for new solutions." As a result, in the local government elections in November 2018, the former ruling camp lost to the environment who gained their political capital in the heat of the fight against the expansion of Opole, but whose election campaign was conducted under the slogan of closing the issue of the commune's division. The activities planned after the elections were to serve the purpose of jointly building a better future.

Conclusions

From the very beginning, social sciences and humanities in their modern forms have taken up the issue of emotions, considering them as an important link between what is "individual" and what is "social." However, only the last decades have brought about the problematization of the premises of earlier studies assuming that "individuals" and "society" constitute mutually forming antinomies in which emotions are "naturally" anchored. By pointing to their material, social, and psychological dimensions, numerous researchers began to increasingly treat emotions as agents (re)producing realities and collective subjects operating within them (Ahmed 2014: 8–12, 44–49). An important aspect of this new approach was the focus on creating, negotiating, and contesting diverse types of solidarity, as well as relations of domination and resistance, which revealed that emotions are usually highly politicized (Abu-Lughod, Lutz 1990). The "affective turn" allowed therefore for moving beyond conventionally understood politics and the political. Hitherto understanding of human conflictuality mostly in terms of strategic struggles of interests and capitals has been supplemented with an insight into "what matters" to people both individually and collectively (Lutz 2017). To this effect, those elements of the present which were previously relegated to the realms of private and personal have entered the realms of public and political.

The proposed analysis of discursive practices linked to the takeover of several villages of the Dobrzeń Wielki commune (including the OPP) by the city of Opole situates the above-mentioned dynamics in a specific context. The affective togetherness emerging in the field of the political, connected by the temporary unity of the cause, place and/or time, undoubtedly remained framed by capillary power of local and supralocal modes of governmentality, thanks to which the discussed manners of thinking and acting were fashioned in particular ways. At the same time, this togetherness was the cause and effect of grassroots forms of resistance. The most striking facet of the studied phenomena was that both emotionally charged discourses and "addressees" of those communicative performances were changing over time.

Since the analyzed discursive field was associated with the anticipation of an uncertain future, it revealed a clash between the "ethics of probability," marked by fear and pessimism, and the "ethics of possibility," which held to a chance to avoid the expected difficulties and dangers. As "a landscape of discernible ends and of practical paths to the achievement of these ends" (Appadurai 2013: 292), the shape of "possible" was transformed with the changing circumstances. This in turn undermined the dominant concepts of "probable." When the commune's division remained only an anticipated future, the horizon of possibility was determined by the hope of preserving the existing forms of "good life," and discursive practices were constituted by a shared *doxa*. However, when the anticipated future became the experienced present, those practices underwent modification. The emergence of competing *orthodoxa* and *heterodoxa* led to a reconfiguration of affective togetherness and a shift of polarity in the field of the political. On the one hand, what was considered as pros within the *doxa*, and later, the *orthodoxa*, became cons within the *heterodoxa*. However, this logic also operated in the opposite direction: in contrast to "orthodox" discourses of authority, in the "heretical" discourses of ordinary people, the fears of inviable commune have been replaced (or at least unsettled) by the hope that the future would bring new possibilities. All this shaped local politics, where support was gained by the faction taking into account the new needs of ordinary people in its program.

In conclusion, emotions are definitely able to manage social configurations in the field of the political, and thereby, to forge affective togetherness that triggers diversified forms of agency. Such an awareness allows for grasping these aspects of the discussed events in the Dobrzeń Wielki commune, and the emotional dynamics pertinent to them, which would be inaccessible by the use of other analytical perspectives. Furthermore, by locating the "tectonic struggle" between the "ethics of probability" and the "ethics of possibility" (Appadurai 2013: 295) in its center, the proposed analysis goes beyond the limitations of research defined by Sherry Ortner (2016) as "dark anthropology" and "anthropology of the good." Therefore, the adopted anthropological insight does not ignore the determinants of various scales that constitute such an experience of the present over which participants have little influence. At the same time, by revealing grassroots modes of resistance, including the underlying aspirations for a "good life," it works for ethics and politics of hope which let imagining changes leading to a better future (Appadurai 2016).

References

Abu-Lughod, Lila. *Veiled Sentiments: Honor and Poetry in a Bedouin Society*, Berkeley: University of California Press, 1986.

Abu-Lughod, Lila and Catherine Lutz. "Introduction: Emotion, Discourse, and the Politics of Everyday Life." In: *Language and the Politics of Emotion*, ed. Catherine Lutz and Lila Abu-Lughod. Cambridge: Cambridge University Press, 1990, pp. 1–23.

Ahmed, Sara. *The Cultural Politics of Emotion: Second Edition*. Edinburgh: Edinburgh University Press, 2014.

Akama, Yoko and Sarah Pink, Shanti Sumartojo. *Uncertainty and Possibility: New Approaches to Future Making in Design Anthropology*, London: Bloomsbury, 2018.

Appadurai, Arjun. "Topographies of the Self: Praise and Emotion in Hindu India." In: *Language and the Politics of Emotion*, ed. Catherine Lutz and Lila Abu-Lughod. Cambridge: Cambridge University Press, 1990, pp. 92–112.

Appadurai, Arjun. *The Future as Cultural Fact: Essays on the Global Condition*. London: Verso, 2013.

Appadurai, Arjun. "Moodswings in the Anthropology of the Emerging Future." *HAU: Journal of Ethnographic Theory* 6(2)/2016, pp. 1–4.

Baer, Monika. "Social Activity of Women in the Dobrzeń Wielki Commune in Light of Anthropological Critique." In: *Mutual Impact: Conflict, Tension and Cooperation in Opole Silesia*, ed. Petr Skalník. Wrocław: Uniwersytet Wrocławski, 2018, pp. 179–202.

Bloch, Maurice and Jonathan Parry. "Introduction: Money and the Morality of Exchange." In: *Money and the Morality of Exchange*, ed. Jonathan Parry and Maurice Bloch. Cambridge: Cambridge University Press, 1989, pp. 1–32.

Dzenovska, Dace and Nicholas de Genova. "Introduction: Desire for the Political in the Aftermath of the Cold War." *Focaal – Journal of Global and Historical Anthropology* 80/2018, pp. 1–15.

Falzon, Mark-Anthony ed. *Multi-Sited Ethnography: Theory, Praxis and Locality in Contemporary Research*. Farnham: Ashgate, 2009.

Fortun, Kim. "Ethnography in Late Industrialism." *Cultural Anthropology* 27(3)/2012, pp. 446–464.

Goodale, Mark. *Anthropology and Law: A Critical Introduction*, New York: New York University Press, 2017.

Haraway, Donna. "Situated Knowledges: The Science Question in Feminism and the Privilege of Partial Perspective." *Feminist Studies* 14(3)/1988, pp. 575–599.

Jacyno, Małgorzata. *Iluzje codzienności: O teorii socjologicznej Pierre'a Bourdieu*. Warszawa: Wydawnictwo IFiS PAN, 1997.

Lemon, Alaina. " 'Your Eyes Are Green like Dollars:' Counterfeit Cash, National Substance, and Currency Apartheid in 1990s Russia." *Cultural Anthropology* 13(l)/1998, pp. 22–55.

Lutz, Catherine. *Unnatural Emotions: Everyday Sentiments on a Micronesian Atoll and Their Challenge to Western Theory*. Chicago: The University of Chicago Press, 1988.

Lutz, Catherine. "What Matters." *Cultural Anthropology* 32(3)/2017, pp. 181–191.

Lutz, Catherine and Lila Abu-Lughod. *Language and the Politics of Emotion*. Cambridge: Cambridge University Press, 1990.

Merry, Sally Engle. "Resistance and the Cultural Power of Law." *Law and Society Review* 29(1)/1995, pp. 11–26.

Mouffe, Chantal. *On the Political*. London: Routledge, 2005.

Müller, Birgit. "The Misgivings of Democracy: Personal Resentment and Alternating Power in a Czech Village." In: *Postsocialism: Politics and Emotions in Central and Eastern Europe*, ed. Maruška Svašek. New York: Berghahn Books, 2008, pp. 178–195.

Ortner, Sherry B. "Dark Anthropology and Its Others: Theory since the Eighties." *HAU: Journal of Ethnographic Theory* 6(1)/2016, pp. 47–73.

Rosaldo, Michele. *Knowledge and Passion: Ilongot Notions of Self and Social Life*. Cambridge: Cambridge University Press,1980.

Rose, Nikolas and Pat O'Malley, Mariana Valverde. "Governmentality." *Annual Review of Law and Social Science* 2/2006, pp. 83–104.

Salazar, Juan Francisco and Sarah Pink, Andrew Irving, Johannes Sjöberg eds. *Anthropologies and Futures: Researching Emerging and Uncertain Worlds*, London: Bloomsbury, 2017.

Samimian-Darash, Limor and Paul Rabinow eds. *Modes of Uncertainty: Anthropological Cases*. Chicago: The University of Chicago Press, 2015.

Scott, James C. *Weapons of the Weak: Everyday Forms of Peasant Resistance*. New Haven: Yale University Press, 1985.

Skoggard, Ian and Alisse Waterston. "Introduction: Toward an Anthropology of Affect and Evocative Ethnography." *Anthropology of Consciousness* 26 (2)/2015, pp. 109–120.

Svašek, Maruška. "The Politics of Emotions: Emotional Discourses and Displays in Post-Cold War Contexts." *Focaal – European Journal of Anthropology* 39/2002, pp. 9–27.

Svašek, Maruška. "Introduction: Postsocialism and the Politics of Emotions." In: *Postsocialism: Politics and Emotions in Central and Eastern Europe*, ed. Maruška Svašek. New York: Berghahn Books, 2008a, pp. 1–33.

Svašek, Maruška ed. *Postsocialism: Politics and Emotions in Central and Eastern Europe*. New York: Berghahn Books, 2008b.

Wilson, Richard Ashby. "Conclusion: Tyrannosaurus Lex: The Anthropology of Human Rights and Transnational Law." In: *The Practice of Human Rights: Tracking Law Between the Global and the Local*, ed. Mark Goodale, Sally Engle Merry. Cambridge: Cambridge University Press, 2007, pp. 342–369.

Ewa Kruk[1]

Femininities in the Face of Large Industrial Investments

Abstract: The article analyzes (re)constructions of femininity taking place in a male-dominated work environment under the influence of a large industrial investment exemplified by Opole Power Plant extension. Putting the reasoning in the context of findings made so far in this field, it shows how the interviewed women (re)construct their femininity under the influence of strategically set goals. By moving on gender continuum between femininity and masculinity, they can expand the area of their agency.

Keywords: agency, femininity, gender, industrial investment, male-dominated work environment.

Femininity as Discourse

Assuming that gender is a cultural performance, women and men can "play" it in a way that goes beyond traditional understanding (Butler 1993). Women, insincerely quoting gender norms, using, among other things, parodies, or masquerades, create realizations of femininity that deviate from the socially approved ideal. Consequently, they can occupy various positions on the gender continuum, construct their femininity differently depending on the circumstances, and keep it in a state of "fluidity." Views of femininity referring to biological, cultural, or psychological aspects – especially the different roles of women and men in reproduction – determine the fundamental difference between genders (Yanagisako, Collier 1987: 30). An important dimension of constructing femininity is, for instance, the category of beauty, which invokes several disciplinary practices aimed at creating specific behaviors and gestures. According to

1 ewa.krukowna@gmail.com, ORCID: 0000-0003-1610-0754.

Sandra Lee Bartky (2007: 52), everyone is born a woman or a man, which does not automatically connotes being male or female.

As Simone de Beauvoir (2017) states, both women and femininity are "artificial" beings created by men who, tormented by a sense of inferiority, use them to maintain a position of domination. A woman is defined in relation to a man, never the other way around – he is the subject, the absolute, she is "different." Taking the position of "otherness" determines thus the essence of "true" femininity. In fact, as de Beauvoir proves, we are dealing only with the myths of femininity created by men according to which the desired attributes of a woman's appearance and character are defined. A woman who wants to fulfill the cultural hallmarks of femininity must give up independence and agree to be subordinate to male perception.

The concepts of femininity and masculinity are inextricably linked with the issue of the gender given at birth, pointing to their desired realizations. The statement "this is a boy/girl" initiates the processes of "girling the girl and boying the boy" (Butler 1993: 7–8), the aim of which is to achieve the ideals of femininity and masculinity. This is done by "quoting" a gender norm that can never be fully embodied, which is a condition for being recognized as a full-fledged entity. Femininity and masculinity are therefore not the result of an autonomous choice, but a derivative of disciplinary practices aimed at creating "bodies susceptible" to cultural interference, constantly regulated in terms of size, shape, gestures, posture, appetite, clothing, and so on. They are a social hoax aimed at constantly meeting gender norms functioning in culture (Mizielińska 2004: 193; Bartky 2007: 52). The dispersion of disciplinary power related to the lack of a direct supervisory authority gives the impression of naturalness and voluntary submission to the processes of producing femininity defined in this way. Disciplining practices, however, may have two dimensions in this respect. Some women, especially those articulating an objection to normative femininity, may reject socially approved ways of gender manifestation. Others, in turn, may experience agency resulting from moving in the space of well-recognized codes and behaviors, while achieving a sense of stable identity (Bartky 2007: 67).

Dorothy Smith (1990: 163 as cited in Mills 1997: 88), treating discourse more as something "what you do" and not what you are subordinated to, recognizes femininity as a discourse entangled in relations of power, but not exclusively subject to it. Femininity does not have one universal meaning, but it is each time a derivative of a series of contextual dependencies, such as position within the hierarchy of power, knowledge, pleasure, or age. This requires connoting the necessity to apply an intersectional approach, where individual categories remain in dynamic relations, intertwining and "disturbing" each other (Crenshaw 1991). The most important aspect in perceiving femininity as a discourse is drawing attention to the individual activity of women, thanks to which they cease to be subject to ideology, but they become conscious creators of their own fate, even in a situation of manifesting femininity in line with cultural recommendations. In this sense, femininity is not an oppressive system, but a type of social organization that is constantly changing, it is, like gender, something we think and something we do.

By rejecting essential definitions and recognizing the sociocultural dimension of the category of femininity, it becomes possible to see the processes of (re)construction of femininity. In this chapter I analyze the above issue with all its context-dependent complexities as exemplified by women working at the construction site of the Opole Power Plant (OPP) extension taking place between 2014 and 2019 in the Dobrzeń Wielki commune in the Opole Silesia region in southwestern Poland. At the time of research, it was one of the largest investments in the energy sector in Europe.[2] The proposed analysis is an attempt to reject the static approach to the category of femininity and to recognize its dynamic, contextual, and discursive character. Women employed at this large industrial investment (re)construct their femininity in a way that responds to the interactions and phenomena they experience in the workplace. Depending on their particular interests and with the aim of gaining male acceptance, they develop strategies to minimize gender-related inconveniences, although the OPP

2 This study was a part of the team research project entitled *Conflict, Tension and Cooperation: A Case Study of Mutual Impact between the Opole Power Plant and the Community of Dobrzeń Wielki*, implemented from August 2014 to January 2019 at the University of Wroclaw with Petr Skalník as the Principal Investigator, and financed by the National Science Center, grant number 2013/11/b/HS3/03895.

extension itself appears to be an area of manifesting femininity and masculinity in their colloquial, essentialist dimensions. Based on specific stories that give the opportunity to place reflections in ethnographic detail, an attempt was made to show how the local and individual finds itself in a clash with the supra-individual. Individual (re)constructions of femininity are a function of intersectionality which is experienced by interviewees, which can take various forms even in a short period of time (at home, at work, etc.), where class, age and position in the employee hierarchy are also important factors.

Women in Male-Dominated Workplace

Women do not form a uniform category and each of them experiences gender in their own way in the workplace. Industrialized occupational areas, traditionally perceived as masculine and generally characterized by different patterns of segregation with respect to gender, show such regularity that each of them is in some way segregated or same-gender. However, gender is only one of many possible negative factors that may intersect with such categories as, among other things, age, "race," class, or sexual orientation. Despite the development of reflection on the diversity of female experience, the research conducted in this field indicates the existence of systematic modes and patterns of discrimination based on gender (Bagilhole 2002: 10–11). Segregation of occupational areas in this regard is the key to maintain gender inequality, influencing pay level, working time, position in the employee hierarchy and access to organizational structures of the company, and is durable despite technological advances in the field of work organization. The literature on the subject distinguishes two dimensions of the classification of occupational areas by gender: horizontal, referring to the domination of one of the genders in certain professions, which results in the recognition of some of them as masculine and some as feminine; and vertical, referring to the situation of women and men employed in a given sector, where women usually occupy lower positions than men, even when they are outnumbered. Both types of segregation have different consequences for women and men. Women are usually employed temporarily, for lower wages than men, and they are also usually subordinate to the men in the employee hierarchy. Men, on the other hand, earn more, usually have the security of long-term employment, and are supervisors of women in the workplace or have with them limited contact (Anker 1997; Bagilhole 2002: 12–13).

The gender segregation of occupational areas appears to be a highly petrified state, despite the implementation of official policies to reduce gender inequalities or campaigns to encourage girls to study at technical faculties. According to Barbara Bagilhole (2002: 24), one cannot speak of a massive encroachment of women into the sectors of work traditionally regarded as male and a reorganization of the model of vertical segregation in terms of gender, but even stronger assignment of them to works stereotypically perceived as female and low-paid. This state is not unrelated to the belief that the existence of the "essence of sex" is true, that is, an indelible and fundamental set of values, properties and obligations that characterize a given gender, which is manifested by the entry of women into male occupational areas only in the absence of prospects for promotion in areas traditionally considered feminine. This process is class-related, and the intensity of women crossing the gender boundaries in this respect increases with the growth of belonging to the middle class. Often important is also the discretionary employment policy practiced by employers, for whom the opening of male labor sectors is potentially associated with lowering the degree of employee integration (Wright 2016: 25).

Women employed in the male occupational area constantly experience "gender labeling." Men often perceive their female co-workers in a sexualized way, which in this context takes on a special dimension, as the attitude of women who treat gender-based pokes not as an abuse, decides whether they are accepted as a colleague or not. In such cases, the distance from the manifestations of sexism constitutes for women a specific rite of passage, including them in the sphere of a male, professional group, thus confirming their ability to work in conditions of high stress. Opposition to gender-based jokes and comments confirms their lack of self-distance and thus the maladjustment to work in the male environment (Collinson, Collinson 1996: 51). Previous research shows how women employed in traditionally non-female areas were forced to show loyalty to the dominant male group (e.g. by agreeing to be the subject of jokes), which as a result strengthened rather than undermined the existing system of gender relations (Kanter 1977). In this context, women can adopt one of the strategies: either they choose to isolate themselves and be excluded from informal friendship networks, or they strive for assimilation. In the latter case, they adapt the stereotypical, often distorted, roles imposed on them, such as, for example, a caring mother, or they become "one of the boys" by recognizing the manifestations of sexism as incidental and showing solidarity with the male work environment (Dryburgh 1999 as cited in Powell et al. 2009: 413).

Women and men are relational, separate but not inseparable categories. In order to gain access to the male environment, women are often reduced to the role of the object of male demonstration, a good example of which, according to Sylvia Gherardi (1994 as cited in Powell et al. 2009: 413–414), is the gesture of appreciation in the form of a pat on the back. Becoming the object of this gesture is an obvious sign of recognition, but due to its culturally masculine dimension, it is also a gesture of devaluation of femininity. Thus, by becoming an "honorary" man, women disqualify their gender. However, by denying a pat on the back, they also reject an offer to join the group. By breaking sexual limitations and entering professions recognized as male, women become "undone" in the sense that their gender is considered an obstacle in their profession.

Empirical Research

In the period from February 2015 to July 2016 research was carried out among women employed in companies forming the consortium implementing the OPP expansion, aimed at capturing the specifics of their work in male-dominated industrial environment. In the course of the investigation, 21 in-depth, open, structured and semi-structured interviews were conducted, mostly with female employees of three consortium companies (except for one case when the interviewee was employed in one of the subcontracting companies) in the ratio of 10:7:2. Usually (excluding two cases, when the meetings took place in the office of an respondent employed in one of the subcontracting companies, and in the area of the extension itself) the meetings took place in interviewees' offices or conference rooms in the container town located in the immediate vicinity of the OPP extension area. The interviewees were people aged between twenty-two and fifty-five, with higher education or still studying, therefore representing the broadly understood middle class[3] and occupying different positions in the employee hierarchy, depending on the specificity of their education. Interesting conclusions were also provided by the participant and non-participant observations made in the circumstances of an interview resulting from being in the "natural" work environment of the respondents and observing the relationships they make in this context.

In the first stage of the research, it was helpful to contact one of the interviewees, who conducted ethnographic field research during her own studies. Therefore, the request for an interview did not cause her anxiety resulting from a lack of knowledge regarding the intention of research, which was frequent in such cases. Although each attempt to arrange an interview was preceded by a description of the project and the chosen method, for most women the situation was so uncertain that without the support of the "doorwoman" many interviews would not have been carried out. Thanks to the above-mentioned person, a group meeting was initiated with six employees of one of the companies implementing the extension project, during which together with Monika Baer, we tried to reduce the initial and natural in such situations distance with respect to "strangers" who want to "carry out research procedures on them."[4] For this purpose, we spontaneously referred to the community of female experiences, bearing in mind, of course, that there is no common essence of femininity that would determine the identity of experiencing specific phenomena. This strategic use of essentialism created an atmosphere of a certain favor towards our research intentions, which was deepened in the course of subsequent meetings. During our next research visits, we always tried to say hello and exchange a few words with our first interviewees, who informed us about new employees and forwarded contact to them.

During the first introductory meeting, the interviewees informed us about the general division of labor performed by women in companies implementing the OPP extension. This included office work, mainly related

3 In this study, following Monika Baer (2003: 19), I believe that the class category is characterized by internal differentiation due to the economic, social, and cultural capitals held by individuals, which in turn is reflected in different discourses and practices manifested by members of a given fraction.

4 The unreferenced quotations originate all from the field research.

to planning, settlements, and purchases; and construction work, which was mainly the domain of health and safety and quality control specialists. As the intensity of construction work increased, so did the participation of women in the entire project, which, practically from the very beginning, according to the interviewees, was relatively high.

The presence of a large investment in a given area, such as the OPP extension, generates new social phenomena arising at the intersection of local and global scales. They usually cause tensions and conflicts which become an impulse for individuals to rebuild their social and economic position, as well as gender-based relationships, because it is the space between categories, boundaries and phenomena that are the area of friction and negotiation of dependencies between the individual and culture (Eriksen 2007: 110). The intensity and size of the investment were reflected in the number of people involved in it, a high percentage of whom, by the standards of the construction industry, were women. This was probably partly related to the generally increased number of women undertaking technical studies, usually reserved for men, and partly it resulted from the transformations taking place in the field of gender relations and the division into female and male works based on them. For this reason, research on the presence of women employed at the OPP expansion was cognitively valuable and due to the size of that project and the degree of women's involvement in its implementation, one can speak of a specific laboratory of gender relations in a male-dominated work environment, which in turn is the basis for predicting the direction of changes taking place in this field research.

"One of the Boys"

The entry of women into the male work environment is a challenge to the ideology of essentialist differences sanctioning male advantage and the "natural" perception of particular professions as male. One of the main questions posed in this context is whether a woman working in a male-dominated work environment is an agent of change or has changed herself? A common strategy adopted by women is to transform into "one of the boys" involving an attempt to blend in with the male environment by emphasizing the similarities rather than differences between the genders and "suppression" for the time of performing professional duties of features considered to be feminine (Wright 2016: 26). In the course of research, several female informants adopted this strategy in their workplace, supporting it with the statement about their "natural" predispositions resulting from such character traits as having an analytical mind and being direct in contacts. As one of the interviewees claims, "generally, I always work better with men, I noticed so, but it may also result from the specificity of the work, because I often cooperated with men in my previous work. They are more specific and ... make decisions easier ... Women reflect, consider various aspects there, and the man decides so and it is." According to the informant, men formulate their thoughts and commands more coherently than women, which does not always facilitate communication at the professional level: "Men, on the other hand, are more specific and sometimes maybe less gentle in providing such feedback, so to speak, what we perceive differently as women. Because we women like to interpret different words in different ways and understand them differently, and men do not attach importance to it." The same interviewee adds that this situation results from the mental overload of women ("they always have a million side matters") and their excessive "vindictiveness." Several informants declare that they remain professional at work, so usually circumstances indicating a gender-based conflict are undesirable, often provoking strong reactions and the need to "bring somebody to the ground."

For some respondents, the impulse to enter the male-dominated professional area was the negative experience of working with women:

> It's fun, a lot is happening and it's a bit different ... I had, I must admit, different experiences when it comes to working with women, and somehow it is easier for me to find myself in the company of men ..., I have already used this term several times: if there is too much ovarian growth per square meter, then the atmosphere becomes highly toxic.

According to this statement, the female environment generates a lot of understatements, conflicts, "babbling," and so-called humors, that is, situations "where one was offended for no matter what." In contrast, contacts with men are easier, because they "lay everything on the line" and "it's nice to argue [with men] – everyone will say what he or she wants and what he or she thinks, and it is forgotten; there is no recollection," men are sincere and open. Another informant states that she even "avoids" women with whom she cannot make contact, because instead of discussing women's topics, she prefers to talk about, for example, an excavator. According to another interviewee, "women are a bit worse than men" because "they are more envious, more unforgiving and capable of worse things than men." Although the interviewees admit that they face manifestations of disregard from male co-workers, they have developed ways of exerting direct and indirect influence on them in order to enable the fulfillment of own duties. In this context, the strategies that women develop to "manage" gender relationships are of interest. In situations of abuse that require a strong response, they often use the masculine idiom of communication. One of the women states that working in a male environment changed her a lot, "because there were situations where I had to put my foot down, because I also have my duties that I have to perform, and I have learned such assertiveness." This sentence was a commentary to a situation where male co-workers try to delegate some of their duties to an informant. One of the interviewees adapted so praised male directness to solve conflict situations and to a colleague, who consciously did not provide her with the information necessary for her work, replied: "I do not compete with you, I only need information and I will certainly not put you out ... of work, nor do I pose any other threat."

The strategy of "being one of the boys" also involves "suppressing" the attributes of femininity, at least for the duration of a stay at the workplace. Women who work mostly with men generally feel that they must be "twice as good" as men in the same position. In order to prove their competences, women performing technical and manual professions often adapt the male style of clothing and practical hairstyle (Wright 2016: 26) and adopt the masculine logic of performing professional duties. Often based on the negation of culturally female characteristics, they make a discursive act of entering the male world. This is especially noticeable in the case of women with technical education who display professional ambitions and a desire for promotion, which is, after all, a common situation. They maintain their femininity in this aspect in an "undone" state, (re)constructing their gender towards masculinity. The informants assumed that when choosing a traditionally male occupation, they had to try more than their male colleagues to prove their qualifications, believing that eventually their gender will no longer matter. In practice, however, as the research of Abigail Powell, Barbara Bagilhole and Andrew Dainty (2009: 412) shows, women recognized as professionals and specialists in their field are also perceived as unfeminine. On the other hand, women representing traditional femininity with the assigned set of character traits, such as sensitivity and protectiveness, are not perceived as effective managers. Moreover, these actions sometimes have the opposite effect – the dominant group of men tends to exaggerate gender barriers and keep women, in such situations, in a position of subordination, because their presence in the area perceived as masculine threatens to undermine privileging them in professional hierarchies.

"Gendered" Body on the Construction Site

In many professions, the ways of manifesting femininity follow certain guidelines. The situation is somewhat different in male-dominated occupations, where the physical differences between women and men are used to justify the low representation of women in a given occupational area. This forces women to balance between femininity and masculinity, which is a specific determinant of a given environment, between their construction and reconstruction. In this context, a frequently adopted strategy is to avoid over-manifesting female characteristics. One of the informants, for example, tries not to exaggerate with perfumes or with a too conspicuous manicure due to male comments. Once, after the New Year, she came to work with tips and heard that one cannot work with such nails on the construction site. Although during the research there was a clear division between women who only work in the office and those who spent most of the time on the construction site, the general tendency to moderately emphasize the attributes of femininity was noticeable in both cases, with the difference, however, that the opposite situation in women from the second group could provoke reservations about their professionalism. However, not all interviewees consider the issue of working in a male-dominated environment in terms of the need to confirm their qualifications in front of male colleagues. An interview who – as she says – "looks what she looks like," that is, possesses the physical attributes of femininity that cannot be hidden, gets "guys cutting her off" with their eyes. But to her it is irrelevant as some "not very clever engineer" is not really respected by her.

One of the manifestations of the gender dimension of their work most often experienced by the researched women are the doubts raised by men, especially the elderly, about their qualifications. One of the interviewees, with engineering education and many years of experience in working on a construction site, recalling the beginnings of her professional career, said that at that time her older male colleagues did not treat her very seriously as a specialist in their field. Only a direct and professional conversation made them understand that "she also knows what she is talking about." Putting into question the authority of women as superiors is repeated in the statements of many respondents. When asked if she often experiences similar situations, another informant occupying a managerial position, as the only one among all the respondents, spontaneously replies "of course." This is especially troublesome when there are specific rules for following which she is responsible for and which, according to some employees, are unnecessary and therefore ignored. When the respondent started her professional career, her male co-workers ostentatiously refused to help her with heavier warehouse work, which, according to her, was a kind of lesson for entering professional area, where "she doesn't belong."

An important issue is the hierarchical subordination of men to women, where lower-level workers especially hardly accept orders given by them. The situation is somewhat different among middle and senior technical staff. This issue should also be considered in relation to nationality and religion. One of the informants, with experience of working abroad, describes her experiences in this area as follows:

> Here in the past also ..., especially when I dealt with employees whom I supervised, where, for example, there were Islamists ... Because I once had such a situation in my profession ... where one of the works managers was Turkish and he said that ... a woman should be at home, right, and cook, not that the woman at the construction site would tell him what to do.

The interviewee emphasizes, however, that she does not experience similar problems in contacts with Polish men who, according to her, belong to the "more tolerant" group, because in Poland women are respected: "[the woman] soothe manners a bit, because they [the workers] have to tutor themselves. They cannot express themselves, so to speak, vulgar." The informant's statement clearly shows the overlapping of the gender category with ethnicity and religion. In the opinion of a Muslim subordinate, it is primarily home that is a field for female activity, and her presence at the construction site, especially as a supervisor, is unthinkable. Such work circumstances force the respondent to recognize at least two cultural codes in order to enable the performance of her duties, expanding the set of strategies she uses: separate for Polish men and separate for representatives of other cultures. In the latter case she usually has uncompromising attitude, because her embedding in the circle of Western European culture, where she usually works, gives her a specific advantage in this context, which is also supported by the attitude of employers.

Moreover, an important factor influencing the relationships between women and men in the workplace is age, especially if a woman's young age goes hand in hand with her higher status in the employee hierarchy. The informants describe the reactions of their male co-workers as follows: "a woman does not know anything about it;" "[a woman] will say some stupid things;" "when I started, you were still pissing in diapers;" or "what do you know?" One of them cites such a situation:

> If you point out somewhere that they should wear these glasses, for example, at a construction site, or long sleeves, because there is a ban on short sleeves so as not to hurt yourself somewhere, for example, especially for those fixers who work on such works, but sometimes it is ridiculed and there are jokes, why, why do you pay attention to me at all, what do you want from me?

The interviewees, especially those with at least several years of work experience, point to the differences occurring due to the presence of women on construction sites. The informant with over twenty years of work experience recalls that during her technical studies doubts as to the reasonableness of the chosen path were sown in women already in the first stage of career development. It was believed that they should be eliminated as soon as possible because "no one will get along with them anyway," as women are not suitable for technical matters. At the time of her studies, the ratio of men to women in her year was 100:3, so it was a field "unfavorable to women." Another one states: "At the beginning I had the impression that … those older lecturers, that they looked rather like that, that a woman is not suitable for construction, and sometimes I feel that I still have to prove something all the time; that guys have it easier. Some may have less experience than me, but they look at him differently because he's a boy." Similar problems were not experienced by the youngest respondents under the age of twenty-five, who in most cases declare that they did not notice either a quantitative disproportion or a qualitative difference in the treatment of girls and boys during technical studies: "After all, it was fifty-fifty. In the beginning there were an awful lot of men, but later it equalized. However, the girls seemed to be ambitious about these studies." Regarding the later work on the construction site, the younger interviewees at first declare that they do not feel treated differently than men or discriminated against. One of them admits, however, that they feel undesirable interest in their physicality on the part of men: "when I was walking somewhere on the construction site, these workers harassed me ... often, really often [they pay attention]." Usually, however, the comments on hairstyle or clothing the informants accept with kindness and even with sympathy. In studies on women working in male-dominated professional areas, the issues of sexual interest shown by men as well as the adversities experienced by women related to their joining the traditionally male area are often raised. At their intersection, the issue of sexuality is shaped, which in this approach is not a manifestation of desire, but a control of women's access to male employment sectors (Bagilhole 2002; Collinson, Collinson 1996; Denissen 2010). Gender relationships with a sexual character are the result of the widespread social use of gender binarism, and sexual harassment is their extreme form. The interviewees admit that there are situations perceived by them as a symptom of gender discrimination. One of them describes her experience as follows:

> These are such situations that I don't really like being judged by the fact that I'm a woman, and they usually treat me like a cute idiot at first. I am already used to it ..., I like to laugh, I have a sense of humor, but when someone comes into such contact ... well, men investigate where the border is. This is a constant procedure, and this limit must be clearly defined somewhere.

Another one, in turn, with an engineering degree, recalls her previous job where in the technology department she was the only woman among thirteen people. The common practice of the company president was to address men as "engineers" and her as "Mrs." as if "she wasn't an engineer herself."

Apart from cases of gender discrimination of an "everyday" nature, that is, often manifested unreflectively in informal contacts at the workplace and free from the aspect of physical violence, one of the informants also mentions abuses of a structural nature forbidden by the law. Being interviewed for a job, she was asked about the fact of having children or possible plans in this regard. The interviewee also points to the existing disproportions in earnings among women and men in the same positions in the company that employs her.

Despite the fact that in many informants' opinion men are easier to cooperate with than women, some of them believe that predispositions to perform a given profession are individual and gender-independent, even contrary to social expectations in this regard: "It is an individual matter, and I would not say, for example, that women are more meticulous, accurate and should always, for example, deal with strictly paperwork, some kind of putting things into the system. I also met men who do it much better and simply feel good about it. It is an individual matter." Another informant adds that it is commonly believed that men are better technically and have a better spatial sense, but her experience shows that women also do well. There were also opinions that their presence in male employment areas has a very positive impact on general relations between employees as they suppress outbursts of male aggression. Correctly identifying the gender codes of behavior prevailing in a given place may be an acquired skill, but the way in which gender is (re)constructed can lead to both increasing and reducing inequalities in this field.

The research shows how the bodies of women employed in traditionally male professions are marked as female, in contrast to male bodies considered semantically neutral and "not requiring discursive legitimation" (Bourdieu 2004: 18). However, women entering the male world do not constitute finite and specified gender beings, but they are looking for new dimensions of femininity in contacts with men and other women (Wright 2016: 111).

Support Networks

The informal support networks established by women in the workplace have a significant impact on minimizing male domination in this regard.

The informant admits: "Maybe women stay closer together, because there aren't many of us, so we also try to meet in private; you talk completely differently than with male colleagues." Contacts with female co-workers, also in their free time, are important for releasing work-related stress, and which are so specific that, in the opinion of the interviewees, only a female colleague from work is able to fully empathize with her situation: "I am not able to tell my friends [from outside of work] what is going on here. They listen to me like that, it's like ok, ok, but if someone hasn't been here, hasn't seen, doesn't know what it looks like, he or she won't understand." The woman maintains intense contact with her three female colleagues, each of whom performs work of a different character, and through the exchange of information each of them can obtain a more comprehensive picture of the OPP extension. In addition, the informant admits that thanks to this familiarity, it is easier to endure stressful situations, which are quickly diagnosed and alleviated. Even though all these "Three Musketeers" tend to exaggerate, through discussing various work events they stabilize their emotions and "they bring each other to the ground." One of them states that a woman working in such a workplace as the OPP expansion site must be open and strong, because the introverted person will be crushed. Another one adds that the fact of working with many men creates a need to balance this state by talking about "typically feminine things." The common custom of going out together to lunch at a nearby cafeteria plays for these informants an important role in transmitting information and maintaining relationships.

In addition to informal, friendly support networks, the informants also established professional relationships with other women working in construction companies that are part of the consortium in order to improve the circulation of necessary information. This network includes mainly employees of the secretariats of each company who have decided to share with each other their responsibilities. If the case does not require "bothering" the management assistant of a given company, a representative of one consortium member herself goes to the employees of the other company to settle the matter. The system includes all potentially interested parties in the circulation of information, even if a formally defined matter is not their responsibility. This is because although the involvement of one of the women is not necessary in a given case, she should not be excluded from the information, because individual actions may be perceived as a manifestation of falling within the scope of someone's competence and this is a matter each interviewed woman is very sensitive about.

The functioning of informal support networks is also important for the fulfillment of maternal roles by the informants. The interviewed women admit that in combining household duties with work, the help of grandparents is invaluable. They sometimes pick up children from kindergarten or school, look after them in emergency situations or take over a greater burden of care when the interviewees take up work outside their place of residence. In urgent situations, however, they can count on the help of their female friends: "There is strength in women, so sometimes I call my friends to pick up [a child from kindergarten] for me, or I pick [somebody's baby] up. ... Without it, it would be difficult. Yesterday I was laughing too, because my friend calls me that she went to a new job and needs to stay longer. I said ok, I'll pick up your son for you." It is an example of developing by the informants a variety of coping strategies and organizing areas of their own decision-making and agency.

Conclusions

The conducted research has shown that in the context of the OPP extension, it comes to the liberation of various constructions of femininity which are a function of age, class, education, and professional experience. Interviewees who are at different stages of their professional career, "played" their gender in different ways. Young female employees, in view of their behavior and appearance, referred to the normative views of femininity. These who already had at least several years of work experience, wanted to function on the principles of male logic. The oldest one, the most experienced and having a relatively high position in the employee hierarchy, recognized gender issue, but their professional position developed over the years had already eliminated at least some of the negative effects of its functioning. The structures of femininity created by the interviewed women in the face of the OPP extension are dynamic, discontinuous, flexible, processual and, to a large extent, also accidental. They take different shapes depending on the experience of women in the context of men's work environment, balancing between femininity and masculinity.

In the above context, after Powell, Bagilhole, and Dainty (2009: 425), one can speak of many femininities (and many masculinities). While such an approach may reinforce hierarchical divisions, it also provides an interpretive framework for the phenomena of "doing" and "undoing" gender. In context-dependent work situations, which are a function of the intersectionality experienced by them, the interviewees activated various aspects of both femininity and masculinity, since these two categories are not exclusively assigned to respectively female and male bodies. By assimilating with male culture through gender performances, the rigid boundaries between genders are weakened, connoting the need for a different view of the issues of inequality occurring in this field. Of course, gender always remains a referential category and it is not possible to analyze the meanings of femininity in isolation from the meanings of masculinity. Every manifestation of gender is therefore contextual in the sense that just as femininity refers to masculinity, so also masculinity constantly refers to femininity. Obviously, the research on masculinity is also valuable and necessary in this approach, especially regarding its hegemonic dimension, which can also be a repressive category for men. However, due to the limited scope of the research being the basis of this text, it could not unfortunately be more problematized here.

Manifestations of gender differentiation are often perceived by women as "natural" and in a way predictable. This is partly because men working on construction sites have not yet fully got used to their presence on the site itself, and not only in offices. This implies the necessity for women to blend in so far mostly male landscape and not the other way around. Powell and Kate Sang (2015: 927) discusses essentialized gender differences in the context of "female capital," that is, a set of acquired competences that are particularly desirable in professions considered as female. In contrast, men have "male capital," which, in common opinion, assigns them to specific male occupations. The informants naturalized male professional predispositions, which in their opinion appeared to be inborn, in contrast to the female predispositions, which are perceived as acquired. It therefore seems that their attitude of adopting a male style of work and becoming "one of the boys" discursively proves that they define themselves in opposition to other women, because of having male occupational competencies and the ability to survive in a male dominated environment. The interviewees admitted that there is a division between them into employees assigned to office work, which in many statements appears to be boring and unchallenging, and employees, who carry out work directly related to the construction, which is dynamic, unpredictable and guarantees a multitude of stimuli. This kind of competition between women creates a "new form of class differentiation" derived from the culture of individualization (McRobbie 2004: 106 as cited in Powell, Sang 2015: 927). Likewise, gender-based behavior is seen rather because of individual choice and is not embedded in the broader context of social relationships. This is well illustrated by Laura A. Rhoton's (2011: 711–712) research among female scientists who distance themselves from stereotypically perceived femininity in their work, striving to meet the seemingly gender-neutral "ideal of the scientist." By identifying femininity with excessive emotionality and the lack of objectivity, they not only make an act of discursive separation from those of their female co-workers who suffer the negative effects of gender, but also contribute to the strengthening of gender inequalities, shifting the burden of responsibility in this respect onto the individual.

In the context of Bourdieu's thought, the strategy of becoming "one of the boys" may be perceived as a manifestation of acting in accordance with the normalized and recognized habitus understood as a set of values and dispositions regarding – in this case – the construction site. In this field "suppressing" the sign of otherness in the form of gender may have a more liberating effect than its overt manifestation (Powell, Sang 2015: 930). In his concept of the habitus, Bourdieu (2007: 193), referring to the intentional actions of an individual endowed with agency, for which the background is cultural reality where these practices are generated, recognizes the possibility of an active confrontation of an individual with adversities, "even if [they] appear to be determined by the future." The (re)constructions of femininity taking place in such circumstances do not need to undermine the *status quo*. Just like in the case of discussed "female" respondents, through the skillful use of social normative rules and expectations, women can gain a sense of a stable identity, to fulfill their own professional ambitions, and find their place in the traditionally unfeminine employment area. The research also made it possible to observe small and subtle acts of resistance and "shifts" in the available constructions of femininity, which for the female informants are certainly a safe form of implementing their own intentions, often contrary to current practices. An example of such activities are informal women's support networks, established to provide childcare and to counteract exclusion from access to information among employees of the secretariats of the consortium companies. Thanks to this, the female interlocutors fight against symbolic violence resulting from the lack of social capital in the workplace in relation to their male co-workers (Powell, Sang 2015: 931). The situation of women, located on the gender continuum between femininity and masculinity, who wants to expand the area of their own agency is summed up by the older interviewee: "A woman must always predict what will happen" and how to outsmart the "powerful," those "on whom no one will pounce."

References

Anker, Richard. "Theories of Occupational Segregation by Sex: An Overview." *International Labour Review* 136 (3)/1997, pp. 315–339.

Baer, Monika. *Women's Spaces: Class, Gender, and the Club: An Anthropological Study of the Transitional Process in Poland.* Wrocław: Wydawnictwo Uniwersytetu Wrocławskiego, 2003.

Bagilhole, Barbara. *Women in Non-Traditional Occupations: Challenging Men.* New York: Palgrave Macmillan, 2002.

Bartky, Sandra Lee. "Foucault, kobiecość i unowocześnienie władzy patriarchalnej." In: *Gender: Perspektywa antropologiczna*, Vol. 2, ed. Renata Ewa Hryciuk, Agnieszka Kościańska. Warszawa: Wydawnictwa Uniwersytetu Warszawskiego, 2007, pp. 50–75.

Beauvoir, Simone de. *Druga płeć.* Warszawa: Czarna Owca, 2017.

Bourdieu, Pierre. *Męska dominacja.* Warszawa: Oficyna Naukowa, 2004.

Bourdieu, Pierre. *Szkic teorii praktyki poprzedzony trzema studiami na temat etnologii Kabylów.* Kęty: Marek Derewiecki, 2007.

Butler, Judith. *Bodies that Matter: On the Discursive Limits of "Sex."* London: Routledge, 1993.

Collinson, Margaret and David Collinson. " 'It's only Dick:' The Sexual Harassment of Women Managers in Insurance Sales." *Work Employment Society* 10(1)/1996, pp. 29–56.

Crenshaw, Kimberle. "Mapping the Margins: Intersectionality, Identity Politics, and Violence Against Women of Color." *Stanford Law Review* 43/1991, pp. 1241–1299.

Denissen, Amy M. "Crossing the Line: How Women in the Building Trades Interpret and Respond to Sexual Conduct at Work." *Journal of Contemporary Ethnography* 39(3)/ 2010, pp. 297–327.

Dryburgh, Heather. "Work Hard, Play Hard: Women and Professionalization in Engineering – Adapting to the Culture." *Gender and Society* 13(5)/1999, pp. 664–682.

Eriksen, Thomas Hylland. *Globalization: The Key Concepts*. Oxford: Berg, 2007.

Gherardi, Silvia. "The Gender We Think, the Gender We Do in Our Everyday Lives." *Human Relations* 47(6)/1994, pp. 591–610.

Kanter, Rosabeth Moss. *Men and Women of the Corporation*. New York: Basic Books, 1977.

McRobbie, Angela. "Notes on 'What Not to Wear' and Post-feminist Symbolic Violence." *The Sociological Review* 52(2)/2004, pp. 97–109.

Mills, Sara. *Discourse: The New Critical Idiom*. London: Routledge, 1997.

Mizielińska, Joanna. *(De)konstrukcje kobiecości: Podmiot feminizmu a problem wykluczenia*. Gdańsk: Słowo/obraz terytoria, 2004.

Powell, Abigail and Barbara Bagilhole, Andre Dainty. "How Women Engineers Do and Undo Gender: Consequences for Gender Equality." *Gender, Work and Organization* 16(4)/2009, pp. 411–428.

Powell, Abigail and Kate Sang. "Everyday Experiences of Sexism in Male-dominated Professions: A Bourdieusian Perspective." *Sociology* 49(5)/2015: 919–936.

Rhoton, Laura A. "Distancing as a Gendered Barrier: Understanding Women Scientists' Gender Practices." *Gender & Society* 25(6)/2011, pp. 696–716.

Smith, Dorothy E. *Texts, Facts and Femininity: Exploring the Relations of Ruling*. London: Routledge, 1990.

Wright, Tessa. *Gender and Sexuality in Male-Dominated Occupations: Women Working in Construction and Transport*. London: Palgrave Macmillan, 2016.

Yanagisako, Sylvia Junko and Jane Fishburne Collier. "Toward a Unified Analysis of Gender and Kinship." In: *Gender and Kinship: Essays Toward Unified Analysis*, ed. Jane Fishburne Collier and Sylvia Junko Yanagisako. Stanford: Stanford University Press, 1987, pp. 14–50.

Marek Pawlak[1]

Mobility, Affects, and Agency in Late Industrialism

Abstract: The chapter aims to analyze the relationship between mobility, affects and agency in the context of late industrialism. It focuses on the affective, spatial, and temporal aspects of mobile lives of the construction workers working on the expansion of the two new blocks of Opole Power Plant in the commune of Dobrzeń Wielki. By drawing on the ethnographic fieldwork at the power plant, the chapter highlights the ways mobile construction workers attune to and deal with their dwellings at the industrial site as well as points out the affective entanglements between future orientations, neoliberalism, and late industrialism.

Key words: affects, agency, future orientation, late industrialism, temporalities.

Introduction

According to Kim Fortun (2012, 2014) ours is an era of late industrialism. We thus live in a time of complex entanglements, which affect our localities, induce various emotions and affects, and inform our social understandings and actions. It is a time of global assemblages (Ong, Collier 2005), which "can refer to a subjective state of cognition and experience of society and culture in movement from a recent past toward a near future (the temporal span of emergence)," as well as "objective relations, a material, structure-like formation, a describable product of emergent social conditions, a configuration of relationships among diverse sites and things" (Marcus, Saka 2006: 102). In other words, the global assemblages of late industrialism create conditions, in which government and business, culture and politics, nature and science, intersect and impact the lived experiences of localities across the world. As such, they often induce dangers, risks, and uncertainties, which must be dealt with on a daily basis. Being a fundamental aspect

1 Institute of Ethnology and Cultural Anthropology, Jagiellonian University in Cracow, marek.pawlak@uj.edu.pl, ORCID: 0000-0002-0396-9154.

of late industrialism, global assemblages might be negotiated or contested by affective agency, which in turn introduces particular understandings of spatial and temporal dynamic.

Fortun (2012: 446) argues that late industrialism began on December 3, 1984, when the world witnessed a "system failure" and a forty-ton tank "released its contents into the air of a sleeping city" of Bhopal in India. This is obviously a symbolic beginning, but with a real-life and disastrous consequences, which cost lives of thousands of people with hundreds of thousands more being exposed to chemical toxins (see Fortun 2001). For Fortun, Bhopal disaster was a peaking point in a shifting world, where the old, industrial infrastructure began to fail in both, literally and metaphorically. In this sense, late industrialism describes the transformative period, when "tight coupling between natural, technical, political, economic, social, and discursive systems" starts to age and "ossify," thereby resulting in deteriorated industrial landscapes "dotted with toxic waste ponds, climate instability, incredible imbrication of commercial interest in knowledge production, in legal decisions, in governance at all scales" (Fortun 2014: 310).

Living in times of late industrialism means to be living in a world of uncertainties, which present themselves as "discursive gaps" and "discursive risks." The former concern yet inconceivable or difficult to explain new emerging circumstances and the latter result from actions and ways of dealing with them (Fortun 2012: 452). According to Fortun (2014: 312–313), conditions of late industrialism present themselves as a "modernist mess"– an example of unintended consequence of "industrial theory of meaning and value" and "industrial language ideology," which created particular "habits of mind, language, building, and regulation in industrial order that privilege production, products, property" (Fortun 2014: 313).

Importantly, there is a crucial link between neoliberal political economy and the conditions of late industrialism, which makes the future uncertain, precarious and, in some cases, even dangerous and life threatening. While neoliberalism loosens the livelihood certainties and introduce profit-oriented "accumulation by dispossession" (see Lash, Urry, 1987), the context of late industrialism evokes the anxieties of working conditions and the questions of safety measures. Altogether, they create the risky environment, where working force is dispensable. Today, the tensions and frictions arising from the attempts to comprehend the existing "mess" induce various affective speculations about the unknown futures. As Fortun (2012: 450) argues, "the future is anteriorized when the past is folded into the way reality presents itself, setting up both the structures and the obligations of the future. The future inhabits the present, yet it also has not yet come – rather like the way toxics inhabit the bodies of those exposed, setting up the future but not yet manifest as disease, nor even as an origin from which a specific and known disease will come." Therefore, the conditions of late industrialism produce particular temporalities, which unfold the ways of understanding not only the past, but also the uncertain future that is often imagined in the present. This is a rather affective context, which has a significant impact on social actions as well the strategies of muddling through the emerging complexities of the present matter.

In the following chapter, I aim to problematize the relationship between mobility, affects and agency in the context of spatial and temporal entanglements of late industrialism. I focus on the mobile lives of the construction workers working on the expansion of the two new blocks of Opole Power Plant (OPP) in the Dobrzeń Wielki commune in the Opole Silesia region (southwestern Poland).[2] Drawing on the ethnographic fieldwork at the power plant, I thus analyze their agency and ways of adapting and attuning to highly mobile lives and their temporariness of dwelling at the industrial site. In doing so, I recapitulate and extend my previous problematizations of the construction workers' livelihood strategies (Pawlak 2018a) and their lived experiences of mobility and temporariness (Pawlak 2018b). Therefore, in the first section, I briefly outline the context of OPP, its expansion and impact on migration process in the region. Next, I parse the construction workers' strategies of attuning to particular spatial and temporal arrangements, which are a result of their temporary

2 This was a part of the team research project *Conflict, Tension and Cooperation: A Case Study of Mutual Impact between the Opole Power Plant and the Community of Dobrzeń Wielki*, implemented from August 2014 to January 2019 at the University of Wroclaw with Petr Skalník as the Principal Investigator, and financed by the National Science Center in Poland, grant number 2013/11/B/HS3/03895.

work contracts as well as the characteristics of the industrial site itself. Finally, I move to problematize the notion of agency as an affective way of muddling through the late industrialism. I conclude the chapter by summarizing the argument and pointing out the epistemic potential of affective and temporal approach to agency.

Mobility at the Industrial Site

The construction of the OPP spans from 1973, when the decision to build was made by the Polish officials, to 1993–1997, when it was gradually opened in the new political and economic reality of capitalism. It is an interesting period of changes and transformations not only in the political economy of the state, but also in the local community's perception of the power plant itself (Rauziński 1988; Łuszczewska 1993; Lesiuk et al. 2000; Rosik-Duleska, Kusz 2009; Sołdra-Gwiżdż 2009). Over time, the initial anxieties among local inhabitants towards the power plant's construction plans gave way to rather neutral or even positive valorization of it. The main reason for that lies in the impact of the power plant on economic development of the region and its feasibility to lower the local unemployment rates. Today, the power plant is already a familiar and important marker in the social, economic, political and cultural landscape of the local community.[3]

The power plant had also a significant impact on the migration process in the Opole region, which is now a well-recognized context of

3 During my ethnographic fieldwork, in the winter of 2015 and of 2016, the power plant, located in the village of Brzezie, was administratively a part of Dobrzeń Wielki commune. However, on January 1, 2017, against the will of local inhabitants, the commune was divided and a large part of Brzezie village, including the OPP, was administratively assigned to the city of Opole. It was a political decision, which faced strong resistance from the local inhabitants manifested in demonstrations that took place in the Dobrzeń Wielki comune and Opole. In 2016, people began to fight for the power plant as well as the commune unity. Apart from protests, they also organized meetings and public consultations, and wrote letters and petitions to the government officials. For many inhabitants, the one and only reason for – as they call it – "annexation"

migration inflows and outflows (see Jończy 2003, 2006, 2010; Heffner, Rauziński 2012; Heffner, Solga 2009; Solga 2009). The region has also a close transnational ties and connections with Germany, which is the most popular destination among the local inhabitants. However, the new expansion of the power plant led to the emergence of the novel migration trend since it has attracted migrant workers and professionals from different parts of Poland, along with Ukraine and Belarus. Most of them stay in the region just temporary, facing various migratory dilemmas of different matter. Having been contracted for specified tasks, and often as part-time workers, migrants "muddle through" the precariousness of their work, multiple subcontracting, and flexible employment. It seems that the relations between mobility and livelihood in migrants' lives represent a significant changes in the wider economic and political context in which big industrial initiatives reveal the existing complex interdependencies between different scales of the global, the national and the local imaginaries of mobility, affects and agency (cf. Pawlak 2018a, 2018b).

As I have already shown elsewhere, the site of the OPP is a rather specific place of ethnographic conduct (Pawlak 2018a, 2018b). It is a rather closed, constrained, and limited space with visible borders and boundaries marked by the scattered coal heaps, rusting industrial infrastructure as well as carefully planned and organized roads and pathways. However, at the same time, the complexities of the site go beyond its spatial physicality and introduce a combination of different scales of social, cultural, political, and economic matter (Fortun 2012). The site is thus both, open to global impacts and vortices (for example, prices of coal or the discourse on environmental degradation) as well closed and hermetic in its spatial arrangements.

In a distance of two hundred meters from the main entrance to the power plant, there is a workers' hostel, where I stayed during my fieldwork, conversing, observing and accompanying the construction workers in their leisure activities between labor shifts. Interestingly, there was a

---

of the commune, was the income tax generated by the OPP, which from now on will contribute to the city of Opole and not the Dobrzeń Wielki commune.

great flux in the hostel, which stemmed from a high mobility of workers, whose arrivals and departures depended on particular work assignments and construction developments. However, there were also some construction workers, who resided in the hostel for a longer period, spanning from couple to even several months. Most of my research participants came from different parts of Poland – such as Mazovia, Silesia, Lesser Poland or Subcarpathia – and were usually employed in a small or medium private construction. They have been subcontracted for specified tasks by the main building contractor Mostostal, which also supervised the whole power plant expansion. The construction workers with whom I spoke and "hanged out" have been working in welding, masonry, carpentering, or as rebar workers. There were also specialists and engineers, who visited hostel's bar in their lunch time, but their accommodation was often in the city of Opole (Pawlak 2018a).

The hostel was a specific, rather isolated space, away from other residential buildings, with few dozen shared rooms and a bar on the ground floor, which became my main site of research observations, inquires, and collaborations. All the staff employed in the hostel (cooks, cleaners, bartenders, and receptionists) were women, and most of them of Ukrainian origins. The hostel was thus an interesting site of spatial and temporal arrangements, which had an impact on construction workers' daily routines and habits. Furthermore, since their work shifts (day or night) lasted sometimes even for twelve hours, from Monday till Friday (but often also Saturdays, depending on the work plan and progress), they had very limited possibility to interact with local community. One of the few opportunities for meeting with local inhabitants, was grocery shopping in the nearby Biedronka store or Tesco located a little bit further in another village. In other words, the day-to-day life of the construction workers was rather constrained to work regime and off time, which they usually spent in the hostel (Pawlak 2018a). Some of them, mostly the young ones, hanged around in the hostel's bar and lounge after work, playing pool, video games or slot machines. Others went straight to their rooms, where they prepared meals, watched cable TV or skyped with their families. During weekends, some of the workers visited Opole's nightclubs, but most of them went back to their hometowns to spend time with family.

Attuning to Mobile Lives

Kathleen Stewart (2007, 2011) points out that the everyday life, which constitutes of various assemblage of practices, knowledge, and meanings, is always strongly affective. Therefore, as social agents, we continuously produce and experience the ordinary affects, which might be defined as "varied, surging capacities to affect and to be affected that give everyday life the quality of a continual motion of relations, scenes, contingencies, and emergences" (Stewart 2007: 1–2). Ordinary affects, Stewart (2007: 2) continues, are

> things that happen ... in impulses, sensations, expectations, daydreams, encounters, and habits of relating, in strategies and their failures, in forms of persuasion, contagion, and compulsion, in modes of attention, attachment, and agency, and in publics and social worlds of all kinds that catch people up in something that feels like *some*thing.

Therefore, following Stewart, I argue that in the mobile lives of the construction workers, ordinary affects play an important role in the ways of dealing with spatial and temporal experiences of their daily routines at the industrial site. In the context of changing environments, they show how the ordinary is affective and continuously assembled. Furthermore, the lived experiences of the ordinary also point to the construction workers' affective forms of attunements, which introduce their agency and guide their mobile lives between different industrial sites.

Attuning the self to particular environments means adapting one's senses, imaginaries and actions "to potential ways of living in or living through things" (Stewart 2011: 452). According to Stewart (2011: 452), this kind of "living through" becomes visible

> in the generative precarity of ordinary sensibilities of not knowing what compels, not being able to sit still, being exhausted, being left behind or being ahead of the curve, being in love with some form or life that comes along, being ready for something – anything – to happen, or orienting yourself to the sole goal of making sure that nothing (more) will happen.

In other words, attunements are the affective ways of dealing with the lived experiences of the spatial and temporal arrangements and they show "how incommensurate elements hang together in a scene that bodies labor to be in or to get through" (Stewart 2011: 452). Thus, they unravel the contexts of negotiating the emerging predicaments or opportunities, which accompany the everyday life developments. Attunements involve imaginaries and actions, which resonate with bodies, thereby making them significant and affective. As Stewart (2011: 452) argues, "in the expressivity of something coming into existence, bodies labor to literally fall into step with the pacing, the habits, the lines of attachment, the responsibilities shouldered, the sentience, of a worlding."

Therefore, attunements are a crucial aspect of the construction workers' mobile lives, which constantly adapt to the changing social and cultural scenery. However, at the beginning of my research at the industrial site, I found it rather difficult to understand how the everyday life of construction workers' is produced and experienced. It was challenging to observe any kind of agency in this limited and constrained site. Furthermore, the intensive labor of my research participants made it difficult for them to organize any substantive activities in their spare time. The time spent outside the construction site was thus limited to the hostel's bar, a game of pool or slot machines. Initially, this kind of ordinary appeared to me as passive and deprived from any form of agency, which in turn induced a sense of my research discomfort (see Pawlak 2018a, 2018b). However, the longer I stayed in the hostel and participated in this form of "passivity," the more forms of attunements I began to notice. For example, there was one evening, which opened for me the research possibilities to problematize otherwise passive ordinary of the construction workers. I was playing two-on-two pool, while other workers were either watching the game or trying their luck playing slot machines. At some point of the evening, a wife called one of the workers sitting next to the slot machine. From their conversation, it seemed that she wanted to discuss some family issues. Interestingly though, they spoke merely for couple of minutes, because he ended the conversation quite annoyed and said out loud "mam na to wyjechane." The notion *wyjechać* means "to leave" and *wyjechane* is a slang word for "not being bothered." This double meaning of *mam wyjechane* expresses both, the physical absence (not being there) as well as specific state of experiencing the ordinary in the mobile life (not thinking or caring about something right now). Thus, it is an interesting expression of being temporarily dis-embedded from daily intimacies and re-embedded in the context of work-driven sojourns, schedules, and activities (Pawlak 2018a).

The idiom *mam wyjechane* is, in my opinion, the embodiment of the construction workers' attuning strategies, which unravel the relationship between agency, affects and temporalities. By practicing intensive mobile lives, they must constantly adjust and adapt to changing circumstances of visited places, contracted jobs, and new co-workers. In doing so, they produce particular affective meanings to experienced temporalities, situations and dwellings. Attunements are obviously diverse, depending on one's individual lived experiences and knowledge as well as the social, cultural, economic, and political particularities of the residing place. However, the attuning practices show the form of agency in which the seemingly passive aspects of construction workers' everyday life also become strategies of living and working in late industrialism.

Throughout my fieldwork, I was thus interested in construction workers' ways of narrating, experiencing, and practicing their mobile lives (Pawlak 2018a, 2018b). It became evident to me that their high and intensive mobility is a valuable resource and a livelihood strategy, which enables them to follow the emerging economic opportunities and support their families. Most of the labor workers I spoke with in the power plant industrial site, were very experienced migrants having been working at various construction sites not only in Poland (Wroclaw, Szczecin, or Warsaw) but also across Europe (Germany, Belgium or the UK). For many, the abiding high mobility and short-term work contracts became their livelihood strategy. By moving from site to site, they have accustomed to specific way of mobile dwelling ("dwelling-in-travel") and created particular coping mechanisms. Therefore, this kind of protracted mobile lives and practices problematize the very idea of place and the ways construction workers attune to particular localities.

Thus, my research participants often told me various stories of their work-related mobilities across Poland. Interestingly, they were referring not to the cities or towns they have sojourned and worked in, but rather to particular constructions sites and building structures, such as bridges, highways or skyscrapers, which they were working on. Often, they started a sentence by saying "When I worked on the construction of the bridge" or "When I was building a road." As if places and localities were indifferent, or at least not important and defined merely by the assigned construction tasks. This way of describing the visited places points to the construction workers' strategies of attuning to emerging spatial and temporal arrangements. Their experiences of mobility and constant movement between different localities make their spatial and temporal dwelling temporary and flexible.

There is obviously a complex relationship between collective and individual experiencing of time, which often reveals the existing frictions between different rhythms of different global, national, and local scales (see Griffiths et al. 2013; cf. Wallman 2004). However, in the case of the construction workers, there is also a sense of time, which might be understood in terms of being "in the meantime;" that is between one contract and another or sharing the same time with people, who we do not necessarily know or interact with. The temporal aspects of construction workers' mobile lives and livelihoods entail different rhythms of "institutionalized time" (work schedules and assigned tasks) as well as "waiting" (for the next work shift, for the end of work shift, for the weekend trip to the hometown) and "time passing" (during the work, after the work; cf. Griffiths et al. 2013). However, experiencing various temporalities is not only related to the context of work schedules, obligations, and dwellings in the construction site, but also an important, and often exhausting, aspect of the construction workers' mobility. I was thus told that living from one job order to another is quite difficult, demanding, and frustrating. Furthermore, being "between jobs" and waiting for a contract to come brings economic uncertainty and traps workers into precarious work (Pawlak 2018a).

Interestingly, apart from being mobile and temporary, the construction workers are also flexible in their livelihood strategies. Flexibility is often a result of their "dwelling-in-travel" and thereby has multiple meanings. It is also a form of affective agency, which helps them to deal with particular situations. Put it differently, in order to work, they need to be flexible and move between different construction sites and tasks. At the same time, they must attune themselves to particular conditions and circumstances (housing arrangements or working conditions) resulting from their mobile livelihoods. In doing so, they practice flexible subjectivities following neoliberal identities of "entrepreneurial self" (Makovicky 2014). It makes them resilient and adaptable to a given working condition. Flexibility of the construction workers enables them to cope with mobility, flux, and change. Their livelihood and identity strategies should thus not be understood in terms of traditional and static category of working class, but rather as neoliberal subjects govern by economic rationalization (see Pawlak 2018a).

Interestingly, in the public imaginary, the link between flexibility and mobility often translates into social and economic "promotion" and "prestige," because the existing neoliberal discourse presents flexibility as a rather positive trait, almost synonymous to freedom and change (Salazar, Smart 2012: ii). Being flexible means to have ability and easiness to change and to be mobile. It seems, however, that in the same public imaginary, mobile construction workers are not a "driving force" needed for infrastructural development but rather "silent agents" of industrialization processes, who often face exclusion, uncertainty and even exploitation.

The attuning strategies of the construction workers are both, the result of habituated mobile livelihood as well as their different lived experiences of particular industrial sites. Since they include mobile and flexible adjustments to particular spatial and temporal arrangements, they might also shed an interesting light on the relationship between agency, affects and uncertainties in late industrialism.

Affective Agency and the Uncertainties of Late Industrialism

There is a significant affective context in the construction workers' mobile lives, which helps them to deal with their routines. After all, affects envelope and animate the processes of everyday life. It is through emotions and affects that people often give meanings to "the changing world" and "shape their subjectivities," while constantly "positioning themselves" in relations to other people, objects, and circumstances (Svašek 2012a: 3; Svašek 2005). However, the emotional and affective "self" is not merely "a closed container of passions" or "an entity that simply reacts to forces from outside," but it rather includes "a mobile, multiple, relational being-in-the-world that is captured by his or her surroundings, engaging with past, present and future situations' (Svašek 2012a: 3). Explorations of affect go beyond the traditional binary conceptualization of body-mind, reason-feeling (Ahmed 2004; Lutz 2017). On the contrary, emotions and affects introduce the dialectics between individuality and collectivity, habitus and identity, imagination, and ideology. As a result, they enable to "capture lived experience, emotionality, and perception" as well as problematize "small and large-scale interactivity; intimacy; and sociality, power, politics, and ever-changing material conditions of social life without reducing one to the other" (Skoggard, Waterston 2015: 117).

Affective approach to emotions transforms the meaning and impact of emotions on the everyday life itself. Therefore, emotions cease to be merely individual feeling and unravel their social, cultural, economic, and political nature (Clough, Halley 2007). As such, emotions do matter since they unravel the existing power relations as well as ideologies, which play a pivotal role in social understandings and actions (Lutz, 2017). Importantly, in the affective perspective, emotions emerge in the dynamics of discourses, practices, and embodied experiences that result from social processes and interactions (Svašek 2012b: 9–13). Therefore, the discursiveness of emotions shows how the cultural categories and meanings of emotions produce knowledge about the lived world as well as the relations between the Self and the Social. The language of emotions, their social and cultural grammar, point to complex identity strategies, which reveal knowledge about self and society that may create, maintain, or challenge power relations and thus influence subjectivity (Svašek 2012b: 9). By focusing on the practices of emotions, on the other hand, one might explore their performative aspects and parse the ways emotions are habituated (Svašek 2012b: 10–11). Performing emotions means following social, cultural, and political understandings of the current matters and expressing their lived outcomes. As Svašek (2012a: 5) argues, "the viewpoint of 'practice' draws attention to the performative nature of emotions, in terms of both unconscious, learned behavior and the more deliberate politics of emotions." Finally, emotions might also be understood as "embodied experiences," which point to social functions, cultural meanings and political roles given to corporeality in particular settings (Svašek 2012b: 11–13). This kind of perspective on emotions "explores physical aspects of emotional experience and subjectivity, analyzing the perceptual process of sensation and interpretation, and exploring the multi-sensorial interaction of bodies in space" (Svašek 2012b: 11). Therefore, the affective approach to emotions emphasizes not only their particular cultural meanings, but also social impact on daily relations, strategies and practices. Since emotions are induced by multisensory landscapes and the ways of being and living through the world, they also play a crucial role in both, individual and collective actions.

Agency might thus be understood as a form of affective dealings with encountered predicaments. In the context of late industrialism, these predicaments often result from various uncertainties, which are produced by global economic and political entanglements (Samimian-Darash, Rabinow 2015). The mobile lives of construction workers, as well as their attunements to particular spatial and temporal work arrangements, show affective and active ways of coping with temporariness and livelihood uncertainty.

However, the emerging uncertainties might also be induced by the materialities of the industrial site itself, as it was during my second field visit in Dobrzeń Wielki in February 2016. My arrival coincided with the fatal accident that happened in the construction site few days before my arrival. One of the construction cranes, attached to the emerging structure of the new block, has malfunctioned causing a tragedy. The crane's jib broke down and two workers, who at that time were inside the transport basket, have fallen from approximately eighty meters. One of them died instantly, the other in the hospital. The whole construction was stopped, and 1,200 workers have been evacuated from the building site. The investigation conducted by the Opole's District Labor Inspectorate, which focused on technical issues and workers' work-time management and schedules, resulted in imposing stricter safety measures in the construction site as well as the maintenance control. In the next following days, some of the workers went back to their homes, while others (mostly Ukrainians and Belarusians) stayed in the hostel, waiting for work to be resumed (Pawlak 2018a).

This tragic accident has "charged the atmosphere" (Stewart 2011) and triggered emotions, which led to various affective interpretations and ideas about "what" has actually happened and "who" should be blamed for it. For example, I was told that during the evacuation, the number 1,200 did not correspond to the number written in the construction documentation, which indicated that there are 800 workers working in the site at the time of tragedy. Hence, for some of the workers, one of the reasons was "cutting the corners" and following "deadlines" and "milestone" instead of the safety measures. However, what is significant here, is not merely the case of actual numbers and if they are correct or not; rather, it is the context of existing perils, risks and uncertainties within an industrial workplace and ways in which they are experienced by construction workers. The accident and its aftermath have also produced fears and anxieties among the workers, who were uncertain about their future. Therefore, the Ukrainians I met were worried about their future salaries and healthcare issues. There was, for example, one worker from western part of Ukraine, who did not want to report his finger injury to the employer, afraid that he will be fired. Another one asked me to explain how does the convalescent leave work in Poland and to confirm that he is still eligible to be paid by his employer, a small building company subcontracted at the power plant's construction site (Pawlak 2018a).

Both, the terrible accident as well as the ongoing nonlinearization of construction workers' livelihood, work organization and safety, induce an affective mixture of anxieties and uncertainties, which are dealt with particular, agency-driven attunements. This kind of context shows how affects intersect with spaces and temporalities, thereby impacting imaginations and actions. There are interesting spatial and temporal complexities, which affectively unfold the existing dependencies between past experiences, current matters, and future orientations. They introduce contingent entanglements, which point to important aspects of our "doing" as well as "being" in the world of social, cultural, economic, and political entanglements of late industrialism. In other words, since "we perform a world into being, acting as much upon anticipation as upon antecedent," then in order "to explain how the world works," one needs to "make new connections between individual imagination and social 'facts'" (Hastrup 2005: 11, 16). Imagining, however does not concern merely the "capacity to construct images" or the "power of mental representations," but is also a way of life in a world that is constantly changing (Ingold 2012: 3). Thus, imagining combines spatial and temporal experiences with social action, which in turn is "never simply a reaction to what has already happened," but also "a mode of acting upon anticipation" (Hastrup 2005: 8, 11). Driven by contingencies and assemblages, imagining is about looking forward to what will happen giving the particular circumstances and past experiences.

It is thus not only the past, but also the future that shape agency and gives meaning to actions in everyday life. In the context of late industrialism, the past and the future are interconnected, often inducing risks and uncertainties, which cannot be left without a response. Ours is thus a time of risks, uncertainties, and instabilities, which are continuously negotiated in local worlds and thus reveal different affective forms of agency.

Conclusions

The industrial site of OPP seems to be already strongly embedded in the local landscape of Dobrzeń Wielki commune. However, its recent expansion has fueled new migration trends to the region and generated new economic initiatives. There is a constant flow of workers in the construction site, which is driven by their contracts and time-related tasks. Interestingly though, there seems to be no deepen interaction between migrants and local community. For construction workers, it is just *another* industrial site to which they have been either "assigned" or simple chose driven by economic opportunity. Thus, they are not interested in local affairs and do not engage in any local activities. To some extent, construction workers, residing temporary in the Dobrzeń Wielki commune, are the embodiment of global entanglement of social, economic, and political forces (Pawlak 2018a). They use their lived experiences of mobile livelihood and affectively attune to given spatial and temporal environments.

The construction workers, who create mobile livelihoods and move between different industrial sites across Poland (and beyond) find themselves in a rather ambiguous position of being "here" and "there." For many, it is an economic strategy, which they follow for several of years (or more), and which enables them to support their families. They are local, but only in places where they live with families; while working and residing in different industrial sites, they experience rather indifference, flexibility, and temporariness towards visiting places. Their mobile livelihood has been habituated and seems to become a strategy of "muddling through" the conditions of neoliberalism and late industrialism. Mobile livelihood creates a working context, in which construction workers cannot be place-bounded and change-proof. Rather, it imposes flexible subjectivities, which enable them to attune to different working conditions and places they visit (Pawlak 2018a, 2018b). For the construction workers, whom I have met in the industrial site, mobility seems to be a valuable resource. To be sure, most of them would prefer to daily commute rather then travel to work-sites, but it does not keep them from making the best of mobility per se. Thus, construction workers' mobile livelihood, altogether with a specific kind of temporariness and flexibility, is an example of their agency, which shows different ways of dealing with the existing global forces and dependencies.

The condition of late industrialism, with all its social, economic, and political entanglements, has a potential to produce new anthropological approach to agency and its role in contemporary lives. Therefore, understanding agency as an affective form of attuning the self to particular spatial and temporal environments, gives us a theoretical possibility to go beyond traditional problematizations of social practices and actions.

References

Ahmed, Sara. "Affective Economies." *Social Text* 22(2)/2004, pp. 117–139.

Clough, Patricia Ticineto and Jean Halley eds. *The Affective Turn: Theorizing the Social.* Durham: Duke University Press, 2007.

Fortun, Kim. *Advocacy after Bhopal: Environmentalism, Disaster, New Global Orders.* Chicago: University of Chicago Press, 2001.

Fortun, Kim. "Ethnography in Late Industrialism." *Cultural Anthropology* 27(3)/2012, pp. 446–464.

Fortun, Kim. "From Latour to Late Industrialism." *HAU: Journal of Ethnographic Theory* 4(1)/2014, pp. 309–329.

Griffiths, Melanie and Ali Rogers, Bridget Anderson. *Migration, Time and Temporalities: Review and Prospect.* Oxford: Oxford University Press, 2013.

Hastrup, Kirsten. "Performing the World: Agency, Anticipation and Creativity." *The Cambridge Journal of Anthropology* 25(2)/2005, pp. 5–19.

Heffner, Krystian and Robert Rauziński. "Ewolucja regionu migracyjnego w Polsce (na przykładzie Śląska Opolskiego)." In: *Problemy współczesnej ekonomii*, ed. Urszula Zagóra-Jonszta, Anna Skórska. Katowice: Uniwersytet Ekonomiczny w Katowicach, 2012, pp. 43–62.

Heffner, Krystian and Brygida Solga. "Współczesna mobilność Polaków a regionalny kontekst procesów migracyjnych." In: *Zmieniająca się rola migracji w rozwoju regionalnym*, ed. Brygida Solga. Opole: Instytut Śląski, 2009, pp. 15–33.

Ingold, Tim. "Introduction." In: *Imagining Landscapes: Past, Present and Future*, ed. Monica Janowski and Tim Ingold. Farnham: Ashgate, 2012, pp. 1–8.

Jończy, Romuald. *Migracje zarobkowe ludności autochtonicznej z województwa opolskiego: Studium ekonomicznych determinant i konsekwencji*. Opole: Uniwersytet Opolski, 2003.

Jończy, Romuald. *Wpływ migracji zagranicznych na dysharmonie rozwoju województwa opolskiego (ze szczególnym uwzględnieniem rynku pracy)*. Opole: Uniwersytet Opolski, 2006.

Jończy, Romuald. *Migracje zagraniczne z obszarów wiejskich województwa opolskiego po akcesji Polski do Unii Europejskiej: Wybrane aspekty ekonomiczne i demograficzne*. Opole–Wrocław: Uniwersytet Ekonomiczny we Wrocławiu, Politechnika Opolska, 2010.

Lash, Scott and John Urry. *The End of Organized Capitalism*. Madison: Wiley, 1987.

Lesiuk, Wiesław and Robert Rauziński, Teresa Sołdra-Gwiżdż eds. *Między przeszłością i przyszłością: Elektrownia "Opole" jako czynnik zmiany społecznej*. Opole: Instytut Śląski, 2000.

Lutz, Catherine. "What Matters." *Cultural Anthropology* 32(3)/2017, pp. 181–191.

Łuszczewska, Barbara ed. *Elektrownia "Opole" a środowisko społeczne*. Opole: Instytut Śląski, 1993.

Makovicky, Nicolette. "Introduction: Me, Inc.? Untangling Neoliberalism, Personhood, and Postsocialism." In: *Neoliberalism, Personhood, and Postsocialism: Enterprising Selves in Changing*

Economies, ed. Nicolette Makovicky. Farnham: Ashgate, 2014, pp. 1–16.

Marcus, George E. and Erkan Saka. "Assemblage." *Theory, Culture and Society* 23(2–3)/2006, pp. 101–106.

Ong, Aihwa and Stephen J. Collier eds. *Global Assemblages: Technology, Politics, and Ethics as Anthropological Problems*. Oxford: Oxford University Press, 2005.

Pawlak, Marek. "Mobile Livelihood: Temporariness, Indifference and Flexibile Subjectivities in the Industrial Site." In: *Mutual Impact: Conflict, Tension and Cooperation in Opole Silesia*, ed. Petr Skalník. Wrocław: Uniwersytet Wrocławski, 2018a, pp. 101–123.

Pawlak, Marek. "Afektywne dostrojenia i sprawczość w czasach późnego industrializmu." *Prace Etnograficzne* 46(4)/2018b, pp. 53–68.

Rauziński, Robert ed. *Wpływ Elektrowni "Opole" na przeobrażenia społeczno-ekonomiczne gminy i rejonu Dobrzeń Wielki*. Opole: Wyższa Szkoła Inżynierska w Opolu, 1988.

Rosik-Dulewska, Czesława and Grzegorz Kusza eds. *Budowa bloków 5 i 6 w PGE Elektrowni Opole SA – aspekty gospodarcze, środowiskowe i społeczne*. Opole: Uniwersytet Opolski, 2009.

Samimian-Darash, Limor and Paul Rabinow eds. *Modes of Uncertainty: Anthropological Cases*. Chicago: The University of Chicago Press, 2015.

Skoggard, Ian and Alisse Waterston. "Introduction: Toward an Anthropology of Affect and Evocative Ethnography." *Anthropology of Consciousness* 26 (2)/2015, pp. 109–120.

Solga, Brygida ed. *Zmieniająca się rola migracji w rozwoju regionalnym*. Opole: Instytut Śląski, 2009.

Sołdra-Gwiżdż, Teresa. "Elektrownia 'Opole' w świetle badań socjologicznych." In: *Budowa Bloków 5 i 6 w PGE Elektrowni Opole SA – Aspekty Gospodarcze, Środowiskowe i Społeczne*, ed. Czesława Rosik-Dulewska, Grzegorz Kusza. Opole: Uniwersytet Opolski, 2009, pp. 47–70.

Stewart, Kathleen. *Ordinary Affects*. Durham: Duke University Press, 2007.

Stewart, Kathleen. "Atmospheric Attunements." *Environment and Planning D: Society and Space* 29/2011, pp. 445–453.

Svašek, Maruška. "Emotions in Anthropology." In: *Mixed Emotions: Anthropological Studies of Feeling*, ed. K. Milton, M. Svašek. Oxford: Oxford University Press, 2005, pp. 1–24.

Svašek, Maruška. "Emotions and Human Mobility: Key Concerns." In: *Emotions and Human Mobility: Ethnographies of Movement*, ed. Maruška Svašek. London: Routledge. 2012a, pp. 1–16.

Svašek, Maruška. "Affective Moves: Transit, Transition and Transformation." In: *Moving Subjects, Moving Objects: Transnationalism, Cultural Production and Emotions*, ed. Maruška Svašek. New York: Berghahn Books, 2012b, pp. 1–40.

Wallman, Sandra. "The Hazards of Overemployment: What Do Chief Executives and Housewives Have in Common?" In: *Workers and Narratives of Survival in Europe: The Management of Precariousness at the End of the Twentieth Century*, ed. Angela Procoli. New York: SUNY Press, 2004, pp. 15–30.

Modernity in Question
Studies in Philosophy, Sociology and History of Ideas

Edited by Małgorzata Kowalska

Volume	1	Andrzej Leder: The Changing Guise of Myths. Philosophical Essays. 2013.
Volume	2	Mateusz Salwa: Illusion in Painting. An Attempt at Philosophical Interpretation. Translated by Katarzyna Pisarek. 2013.
Volume	3	Małgorzata Kowalska (éd.): Morales et politiques postmodernes. 2014.
Volume	4	Andrzej Waśkiewicz: Strangers by Choice. An Asocial Philosophy of Life. Translated by Tul´si Bambry and Agnieska Waśkiewicz. 2015.
Volume	5	Jacek Migasiński: Toward Metaphysics. New Tendencies in French Philosophy in the Middle of the Twentieth Century. Translated by Jan Pytalski. 2014.
Volume	6	Przemysław Czapliński: The Remnants of Modernity. Two Essays on Sarmatism and . Utopia in Polish Contemporary Literature. Translated by Thomas Anessi. 2015.
Volume	7	Bartosz Kuźniarz: Farewell to Postmodernism. Social Theories of the Late Left. Translated by Bill Stanley. 2015.
Volume	8	Małgorzata Kowalska: Dialectics Beyond Dialectics. Essay on Totality and Difference. Translated by Cain Elliott and Jan Burzyński. 2015.
Volume	9	Jacek Dobrowolski: The Rise and Fall of Modern Man. Translated by Simon Loeb and Joanna Guzowska. 2017.
Volume	10	Paweł Majewski: Between an Animal and a Machine. Stanisław Lem's Technological Utopia. 2018.
Volume	11	Anna Burzyńska: Deconstruction, Politics, Performatics. 2019.
Volume	12	Adam Olech: The Semantic Theory of Knowledge. 2020.
Volume	13	Dorota Leszczyna: Ortega y la Escuela de Marburgo. 2020.
Volume	14	Wojciech Tomasik: Insane Run. Railroad and Dark Modernity. 2020.
Volume	15	Jan Kajfosz: Magic in Popular Narratives. Translated by Jan Pytalski. 2021.
Volume	16	Iwona Lorenc: Aesthetics and Modernity. Toward a New Philosophical Functionalization of Art. 2021.
Volume	17	Monika Baer (ed.): Agency at Work. Ethnographies in/of Late Industrialism. 2021.

www.peterlang.com

www.ingramcontent.com/pod-product-compliance
Ingram Content Group UK Ltd.
Pitfield, Milton Keynes, MK11 3LW, UK
UKHW041829100926
8556IPUK00002B/88